Twayne's United States Authors Series

Sylvia E. Bowman, *Editor*

INDIANA UNIVERSITY

Richard Hovey

TUSAS 263

Richard Hovey

RICHARD HOVEY

By WILLIAM R. LINNEMAN
Illinois State University

TWAYNE PUBLISHERS
A DIVISION OF G. K. HALL & CO., BOSTON

Library of Congress Cataloging in Publication Data

Linneman, William R
    Richard Hovey.

    (Twayne's United States authors series ; TUSAS 263)
    Bibliography: p.
    Includes index.
    1. Hovey, Richard, 1864-1900 — Criticism and
interpretation.   I. Title.
PS2008.L5   811'.4   76-891
ISBN 0-8057-7162-X

To the memory of
"Souls of poets dead and gone."

Contents

About the Author

Professor Linneman received his Ph.D. from the University of Illinois in 1960. For his dissertation, he chose to work in the Franklin J. Meine Collection of American Humor, which had been acquired by the University in 1954. Focusing on the years from 1880 to 1900, he has been able to infer many of the attitudes and opinions held by the American middle-class male about ethnic and racial minorities, women, regions, social classes, politics, religion, and literature. The dissertation was both a media analysis and a cultural history. Two chapters have been published: "Satires of American Realism" in *American Literature*, XXXIV (March, 1962), 80–93; and "Immigrant Stereotypes" in *Studies in American Humor*, I (April, 1974), 28–39. The dissertation also produced several other articles and notes, sketches about lesser known periodicals such as *Texas Siftings* and *The Arkansaw Traveler*, and discoveries of unknown works of Stephen Crane. Professor Linneman has also published short stories, parodies, poetry, and articles on American language.

Preface

"For still the man is greater than his art," wrote Richard Hovey about William Shakespeare. While that appraisal might not be accurate in Shakespeare's case, it certainly applies to Hovey. Richard Hovey lived and wrote during the 1890's, the decade that was the crucible for mixing the elements of modern American poetry. His metrical experiments, his themes, his use of myth, and his interest in Symbolism identify him as an important transitional figure. He bridges the gap between the older, more traditional poetry and the innovations of the twentieth century. While not much of his verse is remembered today, it is probable that his personal example and critical opinions influenced the greater poets to come.

It was through my dissertation on American humor that I became interested in Hovey. His poetry, which frequently celebrated wine, women, and song, was somewhat risque for the genteel publications, but often found an outlet in the humor magazines designed for a male audience. His individuality and daring pioneer spirit impressed me, and I resolved to know him better to find out why he was different from other poets of the time.

Because Hovey is little known today and because his work is so closely connected to the esthetic, political, and social trends of the period, I felt it necessary to provide an expanded treatment of his life but to do so within the cultural context of the 1890's. The first chapter accomplishes this biographical aim, but succeeding chapters are concerned with a chronological explication of his works. Since his poetry is out of print and since only a few poems appear in anthologies that might be discovered in the best-stocked libraries, I have quoted the major lyrics, so my readers may know what my explications are about. The several plays written about the Arthurian legends are discussed in Chapter 4, which also discusses Hovey's idealistic metaphysics. The last chapter surveys the rise and decline of his reputation during the twentieth century.

The poems from the Vagabondia series are quoted with permission of Dodd, Mead & Company. I am also indebted to Dr. Joe Kraus, Director of Libraries at Illinois State, and to Mrs. Barbara Glenn for her typing of the manuscript.

WILLIAM R. LINNEMAN

Illinois State University

Chronology

1864   Richard Hovey born May 4 in Normal, Illinois, third son of Charles Edward and Harriette Spofford Hovey.

1868   Hovey family settles in Washington D.C.; Richard educated by his mother.

1880   Publishes private edition of *Poems,* helping with the typesetting himself.

1881   Enters Dartmouth College; the youngest member of his class.

1882   Contributes poetry to *The Dartmouth.*

1883   Matthew Arnold visits Dartmouth.

1884   Hovey edits *Aegis,* the yearbook.

1885   Graduates *cum laude* from Dartmouth; returns to Washington and acts in amateur theatricals.

1886   Studies Greek with William Rainey Harper; enters Episcopal Seminary in New York City, intending to become a priest.

1887   Meets Bliss Carman and goes on walking tour of New England.

1888   Lectures at Thomas Davidson's Summer School of Philosophy and is crowned with laurel wreath by Mrs. Sidney Lanier.

1889   Decides to write a series of dramas based on the Arthurian cycle.

1890   Meets Mrs. Henrietta Russell; acts with a touring company.

1891   Publishes *Launcelot and Guenevere;* goes abroad with Mrs. Russell.

1892   Son, Julian, born in France; Hovey joins Carman in Nova Scotia; "Seaward" published in *Independent.*

1894   Publishes *Songs from Vagabondia* with Carman; marries Mrs. Russell and goes to live in England; translates *The Plays of Maurice Maeterlinck.*

1895	Settles among the Symbolists in France; publishes *The Marriage of Guenevere*.
1896	Returns to America to read poem for Psi Upsilon convention; publishes (with Carman) *More Songs from Vagabondia;* also brings out *The Plays of Maurice Maeterlinck—Second Series*.
1897	Hovey persists in writing poetry even though faced with poverty; his father dies.
1898	Hovey writes "Remember the Maine" and other poetry defending Spanish-American War, collected in *Along the Trail*. Also publishes *The Birth of Galahad*.
1899	Teaches at Barnard College; publishes *Taliesin*.
1900	Dies on February 24. Carman brings out *Last Songs from Vagabondia*.
1907	Mrs. Hovey edits and publishes *The Holy Graal and Other Fragments*.
1908	Mrs. Hovey collects and publishes *To the End of the Trail*.

CHAPTER 1

An American Radical

ALTHOUGH Richard Hovey was a *cum laude* graduate of Dartmouth, he could not get a job teaching high school because of his beard, his long flowing hair, and his unconventional clothes. In his poetry, he celebrated the life of the vagabond and organic living; many of his lyrics, like those of Bob Dylan, Paul Kantner, and Mick Jagger, were about outlaws and rebels. He experimented with hashish in college, roamed restlessly about America and Europe, and was a defender of women's rights. But he was not a poet of the 1960's, nor a Beatnik of the 1950's, nor even a denizen of Greenwich Village in the 1920's. In fact, he died in 1900; and he had achieved what little fame or reputation he would gain in the Gay 90's—the decade of the Gibson Girl and cable cars, of barbershop quartets, and of high collars. If Richard Hovey was not the creator of American Bohemia, he at least kept it alive from the time of Edgar Allan Poe and Walt Whitman until Greenwich Village restored it.

Dissent was in Hovey's blood. He could trace his ancestry to the New England pioneers who had chosen to brave the New World rather than conform to the English church. In fact, five of his ancestors had made the "Mayflower" voyage, and they must have regarded the first Hovey, Daniel by name, who did not arrive until 1637, as something of a late starter. On his mother's side, Hovey was descended from Peter Folger, settler of Nantucket Island, grandfather of Benjamin Franklin, and author of ballads that claimed that the Indian Wars were a punishment sent by God on the people of Massachusetts for their bigotry. America has had better poets than Hovey, but few who were better born.

By the nineteenth century, the Hovey family had worked its way to Thetford, Vermont, the birthplace of the poet's father, Charles Edward Hovey. One of eleven children, his story is typical of the ambitious Yankee of that epoch. He worked as carpenter, lumberjack, and schoolteacher before he had enough money to enroll in Dartmouth at age twenty-one. After his graduation, he became principal of the Framingham Academy in Massachusetts, where he married one of the teachers, Harriette Spofford. But he only stayed there one year. The railroads were opening the Midwest, and the great Yankee exodus had begun. They went first as peddlers of notions, supplying needles, thread, and razors for the pioneer community. They stayed to survey the land, found towns, plant elms, publish newspapers, start banks, and hold mortgages.

As Yankees, they had great faith in education, at least in the common school; and they sent back to the homeland for teachers. Charles Edward Hovey migrated to Peoria, Illinois, where he was principal of the high school. Portraits of him at this period show a strong face, a full beard, and deep-set, far-seeing eyes. When the state of Illinois decided to build a normal school for the preparation of teachers, Hovey became its first president in 1857. Bloomington outbid Peoria for the location, and the family moved again to settle at the northern edge of the city, which later became the town of Normal; and there the poet was born on May 4, 1864.

He was practically fatherless in his infancy. At the beginning of the Civil War, Charles Edward Hovey had raised a regiment from his students and teachers and marched off in answer to Father Abraham's call. He saw action in Missouri, Arkansas, and Mississippi; was wounded several times; and got malaria. At home in Normal, Harriette Hovey turned the home into a hospital for the wounded, cheered southbound troops passing on the Illinois Central a block away, and cared for the baby Richard and his older brother, Alfred. Even when General Hovey was discharged, he returned home for only a short visit. He had long suppressed a desire to practice law, and he had decided that the opportune time had arrived to begin that career and that Washington, D.C., was the place best suited for his talent and ambition. So he went there to begin his practice, and Mrs. Hovey took the two boys to her family home in Andover,

Massachusetts. It turned out to be two and a half years before the family was united under one roof.

If Richard Hovey inherited a certain rebellious nature, it is also possible that the environment of his early years reinforced that trait. There was no father to help form the super-ego; no stern commands or harsh spankings. There was only the soft voice of his mother, reading him stories for hours at a time and giving him considerable attention. There is little doubt that Richard was the mother's favorite; brother Alfred seems to have been the outdoors type, more interested in woods and streams than in stories about knights and ladies. So Mrs. Hovey spent her time with Richard and taught him to read at an early age.

When the family was reunited, Richard was beginning his oedipal stage. Suddenly there was a competitor for his mother's attention and affection, a stranger he did not know, one who had the presumption to issue commands in an authoritative voice. What is a father? the young boy must have wondered. The poet's later rejection of established society, convention, and tradition could have stemmed partly from this period. There might be a reason too why Hovey was drawn to Southern poets: any enemy of his father's could not be all bad. However, this resentment was well suppressed because Hovey and his father had a close relationship throughout their lives. Still, the happiest period of Richard's year could have been the summertime when his mother took him to New England. In a few years Richard developed an allergy that made these Northern excursions necessary.

Most of the education Hovey received was from his mother; the only formal schooling he had before college was two years of preparation in Latin, Greek, and mathematics. His mother, of course, had been a teacher and knew French well enough to work as a translator in a Washington office. From her, Richard learned that language and a great deal of English literature. When she encouraged her son to read what he liked, General Hovey grumbled that the boy read too many story books and did not pay enough attention to more serious studies.[1] Richard did develop, however, an interest in natural science and spent much time at the Smithsonian. Nonetheless, his father worried about the boy's lack of discipline: he never seemed to stick to anything. But Richard did stick to poetry, for he read deeply in Lord

Byron, John Keats, and Algernon Swinburne. He felt the historical presence of Walt Whitman in Washington and was
conscious that Edgar Allan Poe was from Richmond, not too far
away. But the biggest influence on him was Sidney Lanier, who
was then living in Baltimore and who had published his *Poems* in
1877. Hovey published his own *Poems* when he was sixteen, setting
the type himself on a small press belonging to a friend.

I *Dartmouth*

There apparently was never a doubt about the college Richard
Hovey would attend: Dartmouth was in his veins, and Hovey was a
loyal son. In his poems and songs about the college, he helped build
the image of Dartmouth. The "Hanover Winter Song" celebrates
the spirit of the Winter Carnival: the drinking and comradeship by
the fire while the wolf-wind howls outside. And in "Men of
Dartmouth," Hovey attributed the strength and endurance of her
sons to the cold North and to the granite hills of New Hampshire;
but he apparently loved Dartmouth better than he liked it. His
Yankee blood had been thinned by his Southern upbringing, and he
longed for the milder winters where the "great white cold" did not
walk abroad. He thought of transferring to Johns Hopkins; and, after
he had graduated, he usually managed to spend his winters in
Washington and to save New England for the summer.

Hovey was younger by several years than the average student in
his class, most of whom were dour Yankees interested in becoming
doctors, teachers, and engineers. He apparently had little in common with their business-like attitude toward learning, and he seems
to have kept much to himself, but he played at times the role of
the Southern gentleman, just as Poe had while at the University
of Virginia. During Hovey's undergraduate years, Oscar Wilde
made his famous trip through America, preaching the gospel of the
beautiful and "art for art's sake." Receiving Wilde in every town
were groups of young men, "esthetes" dressed in knee pants, long
stockings, loose flowing ties; they sometimes wore monocles; and
they always carried the symbol of the Esthetic Movement, the
sunflower. Hovey was the freak of Dartmouth in such a costume,
but the next day he might appear in the sombrero, bandana, and
high boots of the Wild West where his brother Alfred was now
driving a stage coach. No wonder Richard became a campus legend
during his stay.

Although an outsider, he was still not a recluse: he pledged Psi Upsilon fraternity, wrote poetry and essays for the campus newspaper, edited the year book, and took part in a number of mid-night pranks and escapades. He joined his class on a drinking bout in Montreal, and he used on one occasion a coffin borrowed from the Medical School as a toboggan. But he remained a serious student: he read a great deal, wrote much, and won prizes for dramatic speaking. He was the only one in his class to graduate *cum laude*.[2]

The most important influence on Hovey at Dartmouth was Charles F. Richardson, Professor of English. Richardson was not a pedant, for he had spent many years as an editor in New York and was aware of current literary trends. What is more important, he talked about contemporary writers—Bret Harte, George Washington Cable, Mark Twain—in his classes. He was one of the first scholars of American writing, and he worked for its recognition as a distinct literature. Under his direction, Hovey wrote a long essay on the development of democratic ideas in English poetry; and Hovey's later belief that the American poet had the mission to preach the ideals of democracy to the world probably had its inception in Richardson's classes.

That democracy that Hovey so fervently believed in was not, however, liberal enough for him to obtain a teaching position. Although his letters of recommendation were good, his appearance must have paralyzed most principals and college presidents. Nor could he get an editorial position in either Boston or New York, so he drifted on to Washington. He joined the Art Students League, engaged in amateur theatricals, and made the Hovey home a gathering place for young artists and poets in Washington. But he also evidently thought much about religion. One of the facets of the Esthetic Movement was an interest in the high church. The interest was more than an attraction to the ritual, the mass, and the artistic trappings of Catholicism; for the Esthetes were rebelling against the dominant middle-class attitude so prevalent in England and America: the philosophy of individualism, that allowed for brutal exploitation; and materialism, that corrupted the soul.

This excessive individualism partly had its origin, thought the Esthetes, in the Protestant Reformation, which started the idea that each individual was responsible for his own salvation. The historical consequences of this Protestant dogma were a group of opinions (one hesitates to consider it a philosophy) that allowed individuals to do pretty much what they wanted to do without regard for the welfare of their fellow men. This opinion, unless discouraged, could lead to the eventual destruction of man, society, and the biosphere. Matthew Arnold, who had spoken at Dartmouth during Hovey's time, called it "this strange disease of modern life." One way of checking this wild individualism might be to return to the ritual and dogma of the Medieval church and to let obedience, not initiative, be the key to salvation. And if one, who had been brought up in the Protestant tradition and still had family within it, could not become a Roman Catholic, he could become an Anglo-Catholic. In fact, Hovey had been baptized an Episcopalian while at Dartmouth.

And now he was thinking of becoming a priest. In the fall of 1866, he entered an Episcopal seminary in New York, having spent the summer studying Hebrew under William Rainey Harper at Uncle Alvah Hovey's seminary in Massachusetts. Richard was an enthusiastic novice: he wore a cassock and cord, thought of becoming a monk, and had a small altar set with crucifix and candles in his room.[3] But he remained at the seminary only one year; the General's fears about his son's instability were becoming realized.

II *Vagabond*

The summer after the seminary year, Hovey met Bliss Carman, a young Canadian poet. With Tom Meteyard, an artist, they set off on a walking tour of New England, in imitation of the tradition of the English Romantic poets; at other times, they pretended to be *jongleurs*, the wandering minstrels of the Middle Ages, or even knights-errant in search of adventure. But the trip was mainly an opportunity to commune with nature. Carman, judging from his poetry, appears to have been a sensitive naturalist. He noticed the particulars and small details: the coloring of a leaf, the working of a bee. Hovey's attitude was more robust, for he rejoiced in the comradeship. He liked the idea of being outdoors, but he apparently preferred the tavern at the end of the day. Carman's nature was Henry Thoreau's; Hovey's, Whitman's. Carman appreciated nature for its own sake; for Hovey it was a refuge from the increasing industrialization and urbanization. A love for nature, he believed, was bred into the American consciousness. It had not been many years before when his ancestors had had to know how to survive in the wilderness, had had to be able to meet nature face to face, had had to be able to read it like a page of a book. The ideal of the frontier had persisted in the nation's memory, and Americans preferred to work outside in sunlight and open air. Healthy minds and healthy bodies kept the soul free from morbidity. The influence of Walt Whitman was becoming stronger on Hovey, and the effect of European Estheticism declined as he grew older.

After the walking tour ended, Hovey, who stayed in New England, visited resort hotels and summer inns; and he recited poetry for his board and lodging. Whether Hovey read his works is not known; more likely, he read the dramatic staples from Byron and Poe that would display his fine speaking voice. In any event, the act was enhanced by Hovey's costume: knee britches, velvet coat, sash, and floppy hat. He was neither the first nor last poet to use accouterments to sell himself.

He stayed in Boston for a few months, working briefly at journalism and as an extra in Edwin Booth's Shakespearian company; but, when the north wind blew, he headed South. What was he going to do? Over two years out of college, he still had no purpose or direction to his life, other than the seasonal migrations of a water fowl. Journalism, teaching, and acting were not possibilities, partly because he was never offered a job commensurate with his abilities and partly because they consumed the time he wanted to keep free for reading and writing. Yet he could not continue to drift this way. Vagabondage was all right for a few weeks in the summer, but he could not make a life of it. Perhaps his father was right: Richard could not stick to anything.

A chance meeting with the educator-philosopher Thomas Davidson helped Richard. Davidson had sought Hovey out in a crowd, for he had been struck by the young man's appearance which he thought was remarkably similar to Giotto's portrait of Dante. After speaking with him, Davidson was even more impressed; and he invited him to deliver a series of lectures at his summer school of philosophy. The Concord School of Philosophy and Literature had been founded by Bronson Alcott and William T. Harris, the first United States Commissioner of Education (and, incidentally, the employer of Hovey's mother). When the Concord School disbanded, Davidson began his at Farmington, Connecticut; and it featured such lecturers as Harris, John Dewey, and, of course, Richard Hovey.

The good people at Davidson's summer school were probably shocked when they saw the title of Hovey's address: "The Spirit of Revolt against Scholasticism as Shown in the Mephistopheles of Marlowe and the Mephistopheles of Goethe."[4] But he reassured them that modern devils were less diabolic, for Hovey contrasted the Medieval concept of evil with the modern: the Medieval was dualistic, for it regarded good and evil as opposites always working at odds. Marlowe's Devil always worked unmixed harm; but Goethe's, while more charming and sophisticated, was something of a bumbler. He tried hard but never really succeeded. He meant to do his worst, but some power always obverted him and turned his ill intention into good. For Hovey, Goethe's Mephistopheles was the personification of the modern concept of evil. His concept solved the Medieval dualism, and it answered the eternal question about how a good God could create evil because what appeared to be evil was really part of a grand design. Evil was an illusion; people thought something—an event or person—bad only because they did not understand the real nature of the good. At its worst, evil was an irritant necessary to bring good into action. Men would not prove virtuous if there were not evil to overcome.

In future lyrics, Hovey wrote about outlaws and rebels, the sort of people not usually invited into proper homes. He always seemed to be drawn to the outcast and illegitimate—to those who walked in the night, whose habits appeared immoral, whose words seemed blasphemous. But Hovey was basically an idealist, and appearances were not reality for him. These improper people were not necessarily bad; in fact, they were often more virtuous than the middle class who feared them so. They were a part of God's plan and often acted as moral agents. As Whitman had pointed out in "Chanting the Square Deific," the rebellious force was really a creative medium through which God could effect change. Most religions recognized a trinity of lawgiving father, advocate son, and spirit of life; but the rebellious and dissident gods, the fallen angels, were also part of the total theological scene. The spirit of revolt was essential for developing the total plan; it should not be construed as something evil.

The good people at Davidson's camp probably received much comfort from the speech. If of a more advanced social consciousness than the average citizen (and they probably were), they no doubt had been distressed by the many social evils they had seen around them. They knew of the hopeless condition of most laborers and small farmers; they probably knew something about the plight of the American Indian; they might even have been aware that the freed blacks were still living in serfdom. It would have been soothing to them to know that these conditions were not the result of some maniacal evil but were only temporary distresses and that, because of them, an even greater destiny would some day be realized by the American people. These thoughts, while not stated explicitly in Hovey's speech, were implicit in his philosophical argument; and some of them appeared in later poems. No doubt the talk was heightened by his earnestness, his poetic look, and his resonant voice. Anyway, the people lustily applauded his lecture; and, for an encore, he read some of his poetry. At the conclusion, he was crowned with a laurel wreath by none other than Mrs. Sidney Lanier.[5]

III *To Be a Poet*

The event was a good omen. Recognition by such people as Davidson and Mrs. Lanier was encouraging. Perhaps Hovey's longing to be a poet was not madness, yet it was a decision to be made carefully. "It is a fearful thing to be a poet," he wrote in "The Laurel," especially for an American without an inheritance or the security of a teaching position. There was certainly no money in poetry—not even a livelihood unless one wrote sentimental jingles like James Whitcomb Riley—and the acquisition of wealth was supposedly the aim of any American youth.

Although there never appears to have been a period in American history when cupidity and greed were not strong motivating forces, the last decades of the nineteenth century seem to have been especially money-grubbing and materialistic. This period of industrial expansion saw the rise of the great American fortunes, and the millionaire became something of a folk hero whose comings and goings were recorded in the newspapers, as were the social activities of wife and daughters. Andrew Carnegie was no doubt correct when he observed that the average American was not envious of great wealth—as long as he had his own opportunity to get something. Walt Whitman, who had noticed these trends beginning after the Civil War, felt that the material drive was so strong it could not be stopped. Whitman gave up fighting: it would be necessary, he rationalized, for America to create material wealth before it could achieve spiritual goals.

But there was little danger of Hovey's being weakened by the quest for materialism. The dissent inherited from his Puritan ancestors kept him immune from any affliction of the times, and his pose as a Southern gentleman made him reject commercialism. It is not difficult to understand why Hovey might turn to literature as a calling, but the question as to why he felt poetry was his medium is still unanswered. Prose fiction had become the literary *genre* of Hovey's age, and other young writers of talent, such as Stephen Crane and Hamlin Garland, were writing short stories that attempted a faithful description of the actual scene; and they used imagery and dialect in an effort to communicate truth through effect. Moreover, to any sensible observer, poetry appeared passé. The great names were all silent: Henry Wadsworth Longfellow was dead, and Oliver Wendell Holmes, John Greenleaf Whittier, James Russell Lowell, and Whitman were all old men ready to die. Lanier was gone, and so was Emily Dickinson, but no one knew about her anyway. There were no poetic heroes to imitate, for the only poets still writing were minor figures such as Thomas William Parsons, who had served as the model for Longfellow's poet in *Tales of a Wayside Inn.*

But Richard Hovey believed there was a place for poetry in the prosaic and materialistic world of 1890 and that it was his role to keep the poetic tradition alive. The world needed greater elegance of expression, musical rhythm, intense imagery, and metaphor that shortened and condensed ideas and encompassed it all into one memorable poem. In short, the world had need of beauty; and the poetic mission was to pursue beauty even though that ideal was unobtainable. Hovey makes this purpose clear in "The Laurel," which was dedicated to Mrs. Lanier, not just because of the wreath she had given him that summer but also because the poem is an imitation of one of her husband's most famous poems—"The Symphony."

In this long poem Lanier tried to have the lines sound out the different sections of the orchestra. For example, the chivalrous French horns who come to rescue Lady Love echo: "Fair lady, fair lady." But the poem is more than a musical *tour de force;* it is a Cavalier indictment of Yankee materialism: "O Trade! Would thou wert dead!" Trade is not just simply business; when infused with the spirit of competition, it is "war grown miserly." Trade destroys the beautiful and noble; it cheapens love; it substitutes the false for the true. Love can be rescued only by a dedicated spirit of high romance.

In beginning "The Laurel," Hovey praised Lanier as the poet who had shown the way: "Out of the jar of ways that Trade has turned/ Into a mart where Love may have no place/Save it be bought and sold,/A rare fair soul like a clear lamp burned."[6] The calling of poetry was a difficult one: not only was the work strenuous and the rewards few, but the poet had to suffer much unjust criticism. Whoever would be a poet had to be strong in addition to being wise and great-hearted. Even more difficult perhaps, he had to have the persistence to stay with his art even though the ideal could never be realized.

But the poet (at least the sort of poet that Hovey wished to be) had other responsibilities besides the pursuit of beauty. "The Laurel" also communicates an ethical responsibility: it was the poet's duty to portray the vision of the New Jerusalem, the New World rising, the world of plenty and promise, the world that was being tarnished by commercialism and industrialization—the "foul black breath" that the "trade-snake" belched from a "thousand throats." The young poets who were beginning to write would have to destroy this dragon and restore the world to harmony and health. The poet, then, would be the knight of pure will who could make the wasteland bloom again.

IV *A Knight's Work*

Hovey's dedication to the cause of poetry was something of a religious consecration. He regarded himself a priest, and he certainly had to take the vows of poverty, if not those of chastity and temperance. Like other leaders before him, he had experiences that highlighted his dedication. Although one certainly had to be the moment he was crowned with laurel, his real feeling of conviction did not occur until a train ride from Chicago to Bloomington, Illinois, on New Year's Day, 1889. He was the only passenger on the car, he was heading for the place of his birth, and the time and the occasion were ones for resolution. As he watched the orange sun of evening rest on the rim of the prairie, he thought about his life: where he had come from, what he would be. "And I then and there decided to be a poet and playwright, and to attack the biggest problem I could find to undertake, and to begin with a series of six

plays and three masques on the story of Launcelot and Guenevere."7

Hovey's decision to undertake such a vast project in the setting of
the Middle Ages might seem a little odd, especially since he had
such interesting personal material to draw from. He certainly was
familiar with New England, the region that had given Nathaniel
Hawthorne so many stories; and, since he had witnessed the growth
of the Gilded Age in Washington, D.C., he no doubt knew episodes
of intrigue, corruption, and naked ambition. He had just spent some
time lecturing in Chicago, the city that was then stimulating
Theodore Dreiser, Clarence Darrow, and Frank Lloyd Wright. At
the moment of his decision, he was passing through some of the
most fertile farm land in the world, land which only fifty years
earlier had been a swampy wilderness; and his family had been
pioneers here. Somewhere in his past, material existed for an epic.

Hovey may have rejected the dynamic present in favor of the
Middle Ages because he was trying to ride to fame on the wave of
popularity that the Arthurian legends then enjoyed. The Medieval
cycle of stories that Sir Thomas Malory had collected and pieced
together had been resurrected and refashioned by Alfred Lord
Tennyson and set once more before the world. William Morris,
Swinburne, Arnold, and Richard Wagner had also used the myth.
Hovey's spiritual mentor, Sidney Lanier, had edited a version of
Malory for boys; and, in the year of Hovey's decision, Mark Twain
would bring out his *Connecticut Yankee in King Arthur's Court*. The
Round Table aside, there was a great interest in things Medieval.
All over the country lodges proliferated with names that included
"knights" and "dames." Industrialists and merchants, often known
as "princes" or "barons," built fortress-like castles to live in. It is
little wonder that one of the most popular novels of the time had
been given the romantic title—*When Knighthood Was In Flower*.

Of course, Hovey was influenced by the Arthurian revival, but he
had an even better reason for using the legends. He conceived
Launcelot and Guenevere as a series of problem dramas that would
be united by a common theme. The greatest problem of modern
times, thought Hovey, was the relationship between the individual
and society: what rights does a person have that are his own, and on
what issues ought he conform to the demands of society. Hovey was
not escaping from modern life; he was dealing directly with it; and
the Arthurian cycle seemed the best vehicle for carrying the

theme.[8] The legend was as full of unanswered questions as the conclusion of a daily soap opera: can Launcelot remain loyal to Arthur after loving Guenevere; and can she bring herself to bear Arthur's child to fulfill Merlin's prophecy about an heir? And what of Arthur? Will his ambition destroy the happiness of the kingdom he sought to build?

Nor was there in Medieval times the modern divorce that could serve as a partial solution to the eternal triangle. The characters had to face their predicament squarely. Finally, Hovey hoped by using the myth to avoid the confrontation going on in literary magazines known as the "Realism War." There were arguments about the proper subject matter of literature and about the best style of presentation. Often, the idea that an author wished to communicate would be buried under discussions of technique by the critics. The greater the distance he could put between his story and the nineteenth century, the more visible the theme would become. As his friend Bliss Carman stated, "The Arthurian cycle provided Tennyson with the groundwork of a national epic of noble proportions and majestic beauty; it has furnished romantic data for numberless dramas and lyrics to many poets in many ages; to Richard Hovey it afforded a modern instance stripped of modern dress."[9] "A modern instance" was no doubt an allusion to William Dean Howells' novel about an unhappy marriage and a divorce.

Hovey was modern enough not to follow Tennyson or Malory completely. He took liberties with the plot: Sir Galahad, for example, became the son of Launcelot and Guenevere. Hovey made his own characterizations too. Arthur, the father figure, the head of state, personified aggression and domination; his ambition had rendered him insensitive, and he could rule nations but not govern his own home. Launcelot represented true love; his problem was in loving too many. His love for Arthur was the allegiance of a trusted comrade; his love for Guenevere was a tender passion. These loves were mutually exclusive: he could not love Guenevere and still continue to serve Arthur. Whatever he did would be a violence, either to himself or to others. Guenevere felt less guilt than Launcelot, for she had no memories about the comradeship of campaigns. If Launcelot suffered by being torn between loves, she suffered from her frustration. More rebellious than Launcelot, she represented unchecked individualism; to her, state and crown mattered little.

V *The Ladies Fair*

If Guenevere, more vital than either of the men, soon becomes
the dominant figure in the plays, such was Hovey's intent. His
Arthurian cycle was designed to "deal with women in a new way,"
and it would have been obvious to any of Hovey's contemporaries
that Guenevere was a literary representation of the "new woman."
The feminist movement, which had been so strong in the 1840's but
which had to step aside for the slavery issue, had resurfaced in the
1880's. American women were struggling against the convention
and custom that stifled them. They began to compete with men for
jobs; a few smoked cigarets; they agitated for more liberal marriage
laws; and, of course, there was the issue of their vote. Hovey seems
to have been one of the few men of the time who was sensitive to the
need for women's liberation; most males ridiculed the idea.

The popular archetype for the "new woman" was the Gibson Girl;
the creation of the artist, Charles Dana Gibson, she was portrayed
in the pages of *Life*. This beautiful winsome creature, with her
upswept hairdo and curvaceous figure (held in place by tightly laced
corsets), was recognized as the consummate product of American
civilization. She was the spoiled darling of the upper classes; her
father worked long hours on Wall Street; and her mother contrived
elaborate social events to introduce her to the proper eligible mates.
But the Gibson Girl had a mind of her own: she was self-reliant,
independent, and given to multiple engagements and several
marriages. And sometimes, like Guenevere, she was forced into an
alliance with European nobility against her will; for the goal of most
socially ambitious and wealthy mothers was to have a lord or count
or at least a baronet as a son-in-law; and a substantial dowry was
necessary to buy such a husband. Within the space of forty years,
some hundreds of millions of dollars were spent encouraging
marriages that usually ended unhappily. The predicament that
Guenevere experienced in Hovey's plays was not unique.

In the primeval battle between the head and heart, between
calculation and passion, one should let the heart win, advised
Hovey's poetry to the women of his age. One strong theme running
through the four dramas that were completed is the virtue of the
passion of love. Of course unchecked passion will lead to error, but
mistakes have a way of leading to the truth. For example, the birth
of Galahad, the one knight exceedingly pure and virtuous, was

brought about by the illicit affair between Guenevere and Launcelot. There is a marked contrast between Hovey's Guenevere and Tennyson's. Tennyson's queen is selfish, peevish, and quarrelsome. At the conclusion of the *Idylls*, she goes to a convent where she repents for not having "loved the highest." Hovey's Guenevere is bold, generous, and unrepentant; and her love is so strong she would give up anything for it. She does not necessarily love the highest, but she loves the most. Victorianism was dying: the days of the shrinking violet were over.

Another modern concept that Hovey helped form in his plays was the idea of the artist-hero. He took the British bard, Taliesin, who makes but a shadowy appearance in some of the Arthurian legends, and turned him into one of the leading characters of the dramas. Taliesin surpasses the knights in seeking truth; and, in prophesying, he overshadows Merlin. Before the nineteenth century, poets were frequently represented as fumbling men, as clowns in a way, who were certainly not heroic themselves. The personality of Lord Byron changed this concept somewhat, and Percy B. Shelley in his "Defense of Poetry" said that poets were the unacknowledged legislators of mankind. By the end of the century, the concept was developing that the poet was a consecrated man: he was dedicated to spiritual values in a materialistic world and to skill in a commercial age. Such a poet was Hovey's Taliesin; and he helped prepare the way for the artist-heroes of James Joyce, Thomas Wolfe, and many others in the twentieth century.

VI *Mrs. Russell*

Hovey was hard at work on his plays when he met his own Guenevere, Henrietta Russell, a handsome woman who was old enough to be his mother. Like Guenevere, Mrs. Russell was married and also a "new" woman; and her particular interest was dress reform. She was attempting to do away with the tight corsets which were responsible for the fashionable hourglass figure and which frequently caused ruptured stomach muscles. Mrs. Russell and her husband were followers of Delsartism, a system of exercises and breathing control that was supposed to develop grace and poise in speaking and movement. Mrs. Russell's contribution to the system was the practice of yawning as a relaxing device.

Mrs. Russell, a follower of society, lived off the wealthy and fashionable world by giving lessons in Delsartism. She had attracted

the great in England to her lectures, and sensible people found
educational value in her method. She also charmed society in
America; and, when she set up a studio for the summer months at
Newport, Richard accompanied her. Here he had an opportunity to
observe firsthand the American aristocracy and the titled foreigners
in search of wife and fortune. Hovey's compassion for the Guenevere of his dramas increased; he understood now how women had
been made slaves to custom, fashion, and the ambition of others.
The American girl had no identity of her own: she was a doll or
puppet to be dressed and manipulated by her parents. It is little
wonder that Hovey came to regard passionate love as the salvation
and liberating force from the rules of society. Arranged marriages
interfered with the process of natural selection.

But no matter how much one might be liberated from the false
values of society, it was still necessary to remain discreet. Launcelot
and Guenevere did not reveal their affair, and Hovey also kept his
secret, at least from his parents. Hovey and Mrs. Russell were
lovers for several years before she obtained a divorce and they could
marry. He told his mother first and won her to his side before
approaching his father. The General was upset, not just because of
Mrs. Russell's age, her marriages, and her children, but because
Richard was finally beginning to win a poetic reputation. Reviews of
The Marriage of Guenevere were good; but, if he saddled himself
with family responsibilities, he might damage his career. Richard
argued that he needed an intellectual companion for a wife; he had
always preferred the companionship of older women to the
mannequins who were his age; and, as for damaging his career, Mrs.
Russell would be more of a help than a hindrance. Their lives were
bound close intellectually, and she had become the chief creative
force on his work.[10]

He was gaining a reputation, and his work was appearing in print;
but, since he was receiving little money, he may have thought it
sensible to live and work in Europe since the cost of living was
cheaper there and since he would be closer to the scene of his
subject, the Arthurian legends. Besides, an artist had some dignity
and respect on the Continent. In the autumn of 1891, he accompanied Mrs. Russell abroad; she settled in London for the winter
season, but he went to France. In the spring, he joined Mrs. Russell
in Tours for the birth of their son (Hovey's Galahad was also born in
France). But living abroad was not so fruitful or so inexpensive as he
had imagined, so he returned to America.

While he and Bliss Carman were spending the hay fever season in Nova Scotia, they learned of the death of their poetic acquaintance, Thomas William Parsons. It was natural to respond to this occasion with some sort of tribute, and Hovey wrote the long poem "Seaward" in which he used the Classical elegy form, the pathetic fallacy, the procession of mourners (other poets), and the vision of immortality. The central idea of the poem is that striving for fame is the characteristic that unites all the poets of history. Hovey's lack of financial success had convinced him of this fact.

The poem has one basic fault. If Dr. Johnson complained that the feeling of grief in *Lycidas* was hollow because Milton had not been close to the deceased, the same criticism could be made of "Seaward." In addition, Hovey stretches the limits of reasonable compassion when he asks all nature to mourn for a seventy-three-year-old man who had died by falling down a well. But the passages on immortality are excellent, and the opulent language evokes associations of Paradise. It was certainly the best work he had done to this time, and the *Independent*, which thought highly of the poem, printed it on the front page of the November 17, 1892, issue. Back at Dartmouth, the magazine was displayed prominently in the library; and a freshman by the name of Robert Frost, who was temporarily languishing at the college, saw it. "Seaward" nourished his own nascent poetic ambitions, and in future years he sent several poems to the *Independent*.

VII *The Literary Establishment*

Hovey had been able to gain a beachhead at the *Independent* when Carman was editor there, and he needed all the help he could get in publishing. His poetry was no worse than the average written during the 1890's, but many magazines were not receptive to his rollicking protest songs. Poetry was under the control of Richard Watson Gilder, editor of *The Century*, and of Thomas Bailey Aldrich, editor of *The Atlantic*. Through their volumes of verse and their editorial policies, they imposed the standards of the Genteel Tradition on literature. The "Genteel Tradition," the name given by George Santayana to the pseudo-culture of refinement that arose in America after the Civil War, might be defined as "latter-day Puritanism" or as "American Victorianism." In reality, a complex of values held by the upper middle classes, this tradition covered art, morality, and behavior. Today, its equivalent is known as the "Establishment."

The supreme values recognized by the Genteel Tradition were
wealth and property. The characteristics of those acquiring riches
were respected: those who "paid attention to business" and were
"self-reliant" or "level-headed." Those who did not accumulate
wealth were either lazy, immoral, immigrants, or Negroes and
hence undeserving. The Genteel mind lived in the realm of "ought
to" rather than the world of "is." It believed in ideals, perfection,
and the pure life. Refinement was sought in all things; the topic of
sex was taboo; and the habit of referring to the meat of chicken
as "white" or "dark" began because many women could not bring
themselves to utter the words "breast" or "leg."

The virtues appreciated by this culture were continence and
chastity, strict business principles, clean speaking, piety, and
temperance; but one could look in vain for generosity or benevolence or concern for one's fellow man. The purpose of art and literature was to encourage this refined morality, and the function of
religion was to recognize it and reward it as virtue. Government
existed to secure property. And the ideal education consisted of the
Classics because everyone knew that when God had not spoken
Hebrew, he had spoken Greek and Latin. These prejudices con-
stituted the thinking of the people who bought the magazines and
who comprised the audience for whom poets wrote. Poetry was
written by formula to please this taste, and the mood of the typical
book was sentimental: there were poems idolizing womanhood;
encouraging patriotism, temperance, hard work; eulogizing famous
men. Nature poems were popular; and death, especially the death
of children, was a frequent subject.

Many readers had nostalgic memories of life on the farm or in the
village, of picket fences and hollyhocks, of foaming pails of milk, of
horses pulling wagon loads of hay through barn doors, of swimming
holes, fishing poles, and corn shocks. This rural scene was painted
by James Whitcomb Riley and by a score of others. Mothers wore
shawls, read the Bible, and baked doughnuts and pie; fathers
worked hard and feared God; and no one ever got drunk or ran off
with another woman in this idyllic world of the white church and the
red schoolhouse and in this secure society in which the individual
was still important. This rustic verse was a balm for the harsh,
complex, industrial, and urban world.

Such was the type of poetry demanded by the leading periodicals
of the time, and the poet who did not write according to formula was

given little consideration. Very little of Hovey's poetry was accepted by these magazines; he was angered by such discrimination, and his resentment exploded occasionally in satires. He spoke of "The Pedantic" and "Sharper's" and wrote scathing rhymes, like the following one about Aldrich:

> Dandy Tommy, spick and span,
> Struts before the Gilder clan.
> All the Gilder clan bow down,
> For the beau of Boston town.
> What though, like a lady's waist,
> All his lines are over-laced?
> What though from a shallow brain,
> Smooth inanities hetrain?
> In his emptiness content,
> He achieves his ten per cent.
> And, secure in magazines,
> Rules all rhymsters in their teens.[11]

Fortunately, the so-called quality magazines were not the only publications buying verse. There was *The Independent* (and one now sees the reason for its name) and *The Chap Book*, a little magazine that encouraged avant-garde and experimental writing. There were also the illustrated comic weeklies: *Puck* and *Judge* with their big, colored cartoons about politics; *Life* with its Gibson Girl and satires of high society; *Truth* with its chromo portraits of Broadway and chorus girls. These urban publications were designed for male readers, and poets could be a little freer to satirize sanctimony and provincialism; they could praise drink and love. Hovey and Carman both wrote for these magazines.

VIII *Bohemia*

By 1894, the two poets had published or written several poems, sometimes light and sometimes occasional; but all celebrate the freedom of the artist's life, comradeship, wine, women, and song. Such poetry was affected by the publication of George Du Maurier's *Trilby,* by all odds the most popular novel of the decade; for the reading public was intrigued by the Latin Quarter setting, the story about life among the artists and models, and the theme of talent exploited for wealth. New Yorkers went in search of their own Bohemia and found one in the immigrant section below Fourteenth

Street. Instead of dining with dazzling tablecloths and napery, in the brilliant light of Delmonico's on roast fowl and champagne, Gibson Girls had their escorts take them to West Twelfth Street to Maria's, where they enjoyed red-checkered tablecloths, candle light, spaghetti, and Chianti. In this hangout of artists, models, and writers, they might see the colorful young poet with the black beard and flowing tie, Richard Hovey, and he might recite some of his verses as he sometimes did. Although this interest in Bohemia and in the artist existed, it was General Hovey who made the practical suggestion that the poets combine their verses into a book.[12] As a result, *Songs from Vagabondia* appeared in the fall of 1894.

The thrust of the book is essentially anti-middleclass. There is a conviction that those who stick to the straight and narrow, whose concern is security and respectability, are the ones who are lost. The commercial street with office buildings, telephone lines, and cable cars is not the world of reality. The real world is the ideal world; it is the world of the imagination, not that of analytic reason. What is real—what is true, beautiful, and good—is not found in the main stream but in the eddy currents. The scientific way does not lead to truth; the "goggled men" with "dissecting knives" only destroy.

The Vagabonds, on the other hand, are not stifled by convention. They may indulge in any whim or mood they desire. Their intention is to bury custom, frugality, utility, and morality in the wine cellar. They feel close to the fauns, half hidden in the woods, who are links between man and nature. What do they care if others call them mad? They are true to their individuality and personal identity, but the respectable are lost because they have shirked the highest duty—to themselves.

The poets also counsel youth to strive for fame, seek the new, and rejoice in the thrill of discovery, no matter the lack of reward. Everyone should lead lives more in tune with the emotions; humanity was becoming too intellectualized. The emotion of love is shucked from its middle-class husks and revealed in its essence—it is a spiritual necessity, not a comfortable arrangement. The idea is partly advanced that one is alive only when in love and that true love is often found outside wedlock. There is celebration of the carefree life, the prodigal spirit, and the joys of drinking. Courage, daring, and strength are other values praised; and such brigands as buccaneers and outlaws are commended for possessing those fearsome characteristics. Hovey built these rebellious attitudes on a foundation of comradeship, for all things are possible in brotherhood. Comradeship is the greatest of all values; it lasts when wine, women, and song have disappeared.

> Comrades, pour the wine to-night
> For the parting is with dawn!
> Oh, the clink of cups together,
> With the daylight coming on!
> Greet the morn
> With a double horn,
> When strong men drink together!
>
> Comrades, gird your swords to-night,
> For the battle is with dawn!
> Oh, the clash of shields together,
> With the triumph coming on!
> Greet the foe,
> And lay him low,
> When strong men fight together!
>
> Comrades, watch the tides to-night,
> For the sailing is with dawn!
> Oh, to face the spray together,
> With the tempest coming on!
> Greet the sea
> With a shout of glee,
> When strong men roam together!
>
> Comrades, give a cheer to-night,
> For the dying is with dawn!
> Oh, to meet the stars together,
> With the silence coming on!
> Greet the end
> As a friend a friend,
> When strong men die together![13]

Songs from Vagabondia proved to be an immediate success, going through several printings during the next decade. There were a good many reasons for its success, other than the current interest in Bohemia. College students were a ready audience, for they have always been interested in drinking, love, and freedom; and, if the students of that particular generation grew tired of reading the *Rubaiyat*, they could read *Vagabondia*. Moreover, the average reader found much to enjoy. The poems offered a healthy antidote for some of the rhymed sentiment that was promoted by the

magazines. And for readers who liked Kipling and Robert Louis
Stevenson, and almost everyone did, Carman and Hovey were two
Americans who could swing and rhyme just as sensationally and
whose ideas were quite similar.

The volume also reflects a certain sociological condition in the
nation at that time. The middle-class citizen was only too familiar
with vagabonds or "tramps" as they were more commonly called.
Known as "Weary Willy," "Ragtime," "Mouldy," or most commonly
as "Dusty Roads," the tramp was ridiculed in thousands of
newspaper jokes for his laziness and irresponsibility, for his filth and
rags. There existed great public fear of these vagrants who gathered
in their "jungles" on the outskirts of cities and who begged in the
streets. Because they sometimes banded together and roamed the
countryside, occasionally stealing, the responsible citizen saw no
gay vagabondage here but a dangerous threat to property. And
when the panic of 1893 threw millions out of work, and the tramps
formed armies (Coxey's Army from Ohio; Kelly's from San Francisco) to march on Washington to demonstrate, American citizens
demanded protection.

On the other hand, the panic of 1893 that wiped out millions in
savings and investments no doubt helped convince the reading
public that the poets knew what they were talking about. Certainly,
wealth was not very lasting or very durable, and a man who con-
centrated his energies in acquiring it was pursuing an illusion.
Spiritual values were probably more permanent, and one might
better spend his time appreciating nature or following worthwhile
hobbies like art and music.

The popularity of the volume resulted in a sequel, *More Songs
from Vagabondia*, published in 1896. Although this collection
contains single pieces, such as Hovey's "A Stein Song" and Carman's "A Vagabond Song," that are superior to anything in the first
anthology, the collection as a whole is inferior. The earlier publication has more unity, for the songs are directly related to the several
themes of vagabondage. The size of the second volume was increased by including occasional verses written to friends and god-
children, nature lyrics, and literary eulogies—a hodge-podge of
magazine verse that the poets could collect under no other title.
However, the two poets complemented each other: Carman's
poetry is more refined and literary than Hovey's, for Carman was
content to work within the traditional four-line stanza and did not,

like Hovey, experiment with free verse, short lines, or rhyme combinations. Carman's quiet, sensitive, and wryly humorous verse relieves the reader after Hovey's vigorous protest. Carman did not seem to share the intensity of Hovey's radical conviction that those who followed the professions or the world of business were prostituting themselves.

Some thirty years after the *Vagabondia*, the anthologist Louis Untermeyer questioned the worth of these lyrics that Hovey wrote with missionary zeal to liberate his fellow Americans: " 'Free for what' one asks doggedly, Hovey does not answer directly. . . . Free, one concludes, to escape and dwell with Music and Wine, Myrtle and Wanda, Art and Letters."[14] In "doggedly" asking for a purpose, Untermeyer missed the whole point; for freedom from purpose itself is what the vagabond wants—freedom from a practical society that demands everything be done for some useful end, from a materialistic science that dotes on cause and effect, from a Puritanical religion that looks for a teleological thread in all existence. The vagabond has a purpose all right: the search for the highest values. But the purpose is implied and never stated, and it always arises in revolt.

No one is going to confuse the *Vagabondia* volumes with Wordsworth and Coleridge's *Lyrical Ballads*. There are no new esthetic principles applied here; there is nothing especially new in the way of subject matter or style. The poems are basically a protest against the cautious and bourgeois tendencies of American society. A popular lecture of the 1890's was Russell Conwell's "Acres of Diamonds," which told the story of the Persian, Al Hafed, who sold his farm and went throughout the earth seeking diamonds. Ironically, a diamond mine was discovered on the farm. The speech catered to the provincial and unadventurous, by telling such people to stick to the old, comfortable, and secure patterns of life, thought and literature. It was against prejudices of this sort that the two *Vagabondia* volumes were written.

IX *Symbolism*

Hovey and Mrs. Russell were finally married in January, 1894, and shortly thereafter sailed for Europe. Mrs. Hovey's contacts put them into a social whirl, and the couple was entertained by the literati, including Oscar Wilde, who, according to Mrs. Hovey, "raced after Richard all evening."[15] Hovey had already contracted to translate the plays of the Symbolic dramatist, Maurice Maeterlinck; and, when Maeterlinck came to London, he was so impressed with Hovey both as a man and a poet that he made him his official translator.

The next year the Hoveys went to France, for Hovey no doubt wished to learn more about the Symbolist movement in poetry. In art, the Symbolists, along with the Impressionists, were becoming well known—even infamous. The psychologist Max Nordau in his book *Degeneration* assured the middle classes that there was nothing to be respected in these new movements in art, music, and literature that were so disturbing to conventional tastes. To Nordau, the composers were no longer capable of melody; they merely worked for effects. Modern artists had not mastered the techniques of their craft: since they could not draw, they painted instead with blotches, points, and smears of color. And poets had to write free verse because they were not disciplined and talented enough to write in the traditional metrical forms. The modern artists were degenerate; they associated with "low life"—with prostitutes, criminals, and night creatures of the cities. Moreover, they were known homosexuals, alcoholics, and drug addicts. Degeneration had come about, reasoned Nordau, because of the toxic environment of modern life. People's brains were being so poisoned by the pollution of the cities, by the lack of fresh air and sunshine, that they could no longer think right.

Nordau's description would have been enough to recommend the Symbolists to Hovey, but he was attracted to them for other reasons as well. As a practicing poet, he was well aware of the basic problem of whether or not a thing described represented more than itself alone. In college, he carefully and thoughtfully read the lectures of Frederick W. Robertson, an English cleric, which were given in 1852 about symbolism and poetry. Robertson, who owed a great deal to William Wordsworth and Samuel Taylor Coleridge, indicated that poetry is both the symbolic and the natural language of excited feelings. In contrast to science which is analytic and explicit, poetry is the indirect expression of feelings which cannot be expressed directly: "Hence the soul clothes those feelings in symbolic and sensuous imagery, to suggest them."[16]

Symbolism, as a movement, had its inception in the work of the French poets, Charles Baudelaire and Stéphane Mallarmé. It was partly a reaction to the Realism of Honoré Balzac and Emile Zola.

Zola had asked for the writer to be something of a clinical scientist and to describe faithfully his characters and their backgrounds. The poets, on the other hand, wanted to use description to achieve a psychological effect rather than scientific accuracy. They were similar to the Impressionist artist who no longer tried to represent his subjects faithfully (because the camera could do it better) but who used swirls or spots of color in an attempt to suggest a mood or a feeling. Such an artist also distorted perspective and made representation a means and not an end in itself. The poet, too, became less interested in his subject and more concerned about the associations that the subject might evoke in the readers.

The Symbolist poets, then, became more conscious and deliberate in their use of a technique that was hardly new to poetry; for most good poets, especially English ones, have been symbolic, even if unconsciously so. Toward the middle of the nineteenth century, American writers—such as Ralph Waldo Emerson, Nathaniel Hawthorne, Herman Melville, and Edgar Allan Poe—had deliberately developed symbols in their writing. Indeed, the work of Poe convinced Baudelaire that he ought to make French poetry, which was logical and classical, more like the English poems which were symbolic and lyrical. Poe had argued that the poet's primary aim is to create an effect; Baudelaire adopted this point too. So poetry began to move, in the eyes of the average reader, from order to confusion. In fact, Mallarmé, who thought the poet should suggest instead of being explicit, sought a conscious obscurity in his poetry. He used such camouflage as autumn haze, urban smoke, night and fog.

The argument between the Symbolists and Naturalists in France was familiar to Hovey because it was very similar to the "Realism War" in America. The Realist wanted a literature that was true and faithful to life even if it were dull, and ordinary characters facing contemporary problems was the subject matter sought. To the Realists, no more artificial heroes or heroines who engaged in extravagant adventures, spoke inflated rhetoric, and tried to live by absurd ideals were to be created. Authors who were on the other side argued that the ordinary or the dull should never be the aim of literature. Moreover, people liked to read about adventure; they wanted exciting plots and exalted language. They expected the heroes of Romance to be ideal characters who would encourage a higher morality in their own lives. Behind this Romantic esthetic lay a principle very similar to Symbolism: imagery could be a means to an end—and not an end in itself.

Hovey, of course, was more sophisticated than most of the defenders of Romance. He saw the validity of the Realist's argument that communication was made possible by using familiar people and scenes instead of the unusual or atypical. But, as he asserted in an essay with the significant title, "The Passing of Realism," the real or the common should be presented as it actually is: the process or the stage of an ideal development. Hovey's definition of Realism is somewhat similar to that of Robert Frost, who used the analogy of two kinds of potatoes: those with dirt and those scrubbed clean. Hovey's image would not be the thing itself with all its sordid attachments of material life; it would be the evolutionary stage in the development of an ideal.

The association of Richard Hovey with the French Symbolists is somewhat perplexing for the student of literature—his poetry is so unlike theirs. True, he did imitate their style in some "nocturnes," and *vers libre* may have loosened his own poetic line; but, by the time he met and became an acquaintance of Mallarmé in 1895, his own poetic style was definitely fixed. Symbolism was important to him for the articulation and direction it gave to certain feelings, stirrings, and drifts of thought he had been experiencing for years. He had been searching for a higher esthetic and for a more artistic technique than Realism could provide, and Symbolism gave him the critical base upon which to stand. For his part, Hovey acted as a publicist for the movement; and his lectures, essays, and translations did much to make America aware of Symbolism.

X *Dartmouth Lyrics*

Most of the time in Europe, Hovey was beset with financial problems. He could no longer act like a carefree vagabond since, now a married man, he had to provide for his own child and for Mrs. Russell's children by former marriages. His royalty checks were small; and, although his wife continued to give lectures which were well attended and applauded, she was very seldom given any money. Moreover, he could no longer count as much as he had on support from home since his father was aged, infirm, and supported by pension. Hovey wanted to return to America, but he had no money to pay for passage. However, Psi Upsilon fraternity offered to pay his way if he would read an original poem at its spring convention in Michigan.

A reader today might be surprised to discover that Hovey was a loyal fraternity man, but fraternities were something more in those days than the bejewelled Masonic imitations or "prep schools" for Rotary that they became in the twentieth century. Fraternities then were partly literary societies that featured debates, book reports, drama, and comic skits. Hovey's association with Psi Upsilon gave him an opportunity to exercise his talents, but more important in Hovey's eyes was the value of comradeship learned from fraternity life. The curriculum of the college nourished the brain, but the fraternity developed the heart and was, therefore, the nobler aspect of the collegiate experience. Fraternity drinking bouts were not sodden inebriation but the source of dreams and noble ambition, and the forge for welding the dear love of comrades.

This belief Hovey put into the ode "Spring," which was read at the convention. A long poem, its structure follows the progress of life from the period of youth and preparation to adulthood and maturity. The two parts are connected by the lyric "A Stein Song," Hovey's most famous poem:

> Give a rouse, then, in the Maytime
> For a life that knows no fear!
> Turn night time into daytime
> With the sunlight of good cheer!
> For it's always fair weather
> When good fellows get together,
> With a stein on the table and a good song ringing clear.

> When the wind comes up from Cuba
> And the birds are on the wing,
> And our hearts are patting juba
> To the banjo of the spring,
> Then it's no wonder whether
> The boys will get together,
> With a stein on the table and a cheer for everything.

> For we're all frank-and-twenty
> When the spring is in the air;
> And we've faith and hope a-plenty,
> And we've life and love to spare;
> And it's birds of a feather
> When we all get together,
> With a stein on the table and a heart without a care.

> For we know the world is glorious
> And the goal a golden thing,
> And that God is not censorious
> When his children have their fling;
> And life slips its tether
> When the boys get together,
> With a stein on the table in the Fellowship of spring.[17]

But, no matter how much college was celebrated or justified, the average person was very skeptical of the benefits of higher education. What did all that carousing and midnight pranks, football, baseball, or rowing have to do with education? Most people were sympathetic with the farmer, Silas Wayback, when he was told that his son was taking up fencing in college. At last he was learning something that was useful on the farm. College-bred was defined as a four-year loaf made with the old man's dough. The college man was generally pictured as naive and ineffectual; Horatio Alger heroes preferred to work as messenger boys in brokerage offices rather than attend college. Wealthy men who had made their own way, such as Andrew Carnegie, advised the nation's youth to learn the virtues of industry and thrift instead of singing songs, drinking beer, and translating Horace.

There were also educators who were critical of the curriculum. What was the use of all this Greek and Latin? argued John Dewey and Booker T. Washington; education should be more concerned with problems and contemporary life. The popular press adopted this cry in an attempt to make education more practical. America had a pressing need for scientists and engineers; it had enough poets who were writing about the beauty of flowers; and it needed agronomists who understood fertilizing methods and crop rotation.

Hovey answered this skeptical attitude in an indirect manner, mainly in the poems collected under the rubric "Dartmouth Lyrics" that appeared in *Along the Trail* (1898). As any good humanist would be, he was disdainful toward the accomplishments of science. Scientific investigation was perhaps necessary, but the scientific method should not be allowed to destroy nature. Science students themselves were comic, unrelated beings who lived in a strange world of ohms and logarithms. It was much more important for the average student to learn the ways of nature rather than the laws of science. Hovey was following the advice that Ralph Waldo Emerson had given in "The American Scholar."

The real value of a college education was not in the knowledge learned but in striving for knowledge and in learning how to achieve goals. Greek and Latin were perhaps not practical in themselves, but they were valuable for the discipline they taught and for the sense of difficulty overcome. Hovey in the "Dartmouth Ode" stated that college was the time for preparation of ideals; it was also the proving ground for persistence and endurance. For most of such instruction, Dartmouth was, in Hovey's mind, an excellent institution. There was a strong sense of loyalty among the students; the rustic setting and woods were a good laboratory for the study of nature; but, most of all, the rugged granite hills and the cold north wind taught toughness and vigor.

Hovey also had some definite opinions about teaching. He applied for a great many teaching positions, and the applications forced him to consider what good teaching really ought to be like. Referring to one particular job, he wrote in a letter: "I am not to be restricted to English, nor am I to be burdened with anything philological or otherwise apart from the aesthetic idea of spiritual function of poetry and letters. In other words, as I understand it, they want me to teach *Poetry*, not grammar nor historical anecdotes nor any other unessentials."[18] This brief statement contains two interesting points. First, Hovey wanted to teach literature—not just English literature—but European and perhaps even American as well. Second, he was not interested in the approach that would consist of background lectures on the spirit of the time or the life of the author.

Such approaches were then becoming popular in American universities because of the rise of graduate schools that based their demands on the Germanic tradition of thorough research. Hovey was apparently directly opposed to that trend or, as he put it, to any approach that would take away from the "aesthetic idea or spiritual function of poetry." When he did secure a teaching position (for one year at Barnard), he carried his principles into the classroom by concentrating on the poetry itself rather than the poet or the times.[19] Hovey was practicing the pedagogical application of the "new criticism" long before it had been formulated.

XI *War and Peace*

The ode "Spring" that brought Richard Hovey home to America brought him to a turbulent country. To many observers of the year

1896, America seemed ready for a Civil War—a war as sectional as the one fought between the states in 1860–65. The fundamental cause in the 1890's was economic, and the principal issue was the money supply. The farmers of the West and South who owed money wanted to see an increased coinage of silver dollars that would allow for prices to be inflated and debts to be paid off more easily. Naturally, the banks and the mortgage-holders of the North and East did not want to have their loans cheapened; therefore, they wanted to continue on a strict gold standard. The Populist orators of the farm states were threatening to put an end to the domination by Wall Street, by the monopolies, and by the railroads. They were predicting a new day and a new arrangement of things, and Hovey's poem "Spring" contains similar sentiments: he envisions a new world of opulence and ease, vitality and joy, in which all men are united in comradeship. A few weeks after Hovey read his poem, William Jennings Bryan delivered his famous "Cross of Gold" speech which contained thoughts that Hovey, a follower of Henry George and Edward Bellamy, would agree with.

But Hovey's poem, rather than being a call for rebellion, was more for the reconciliation of opposites, East and West, capital and labor, science and art. Men have the same ends in mind; if they could work together in the spirit of comradeship, they could achieve them more readily. For Hovey's vision of evil was not so sterile as the social philosophy of some of the thinkers of the decade. For example, William Graham Sumner had argued that there was little man could do to eradicate social injustice and inequality; therefore, he should not waste energy by trying. But evil, for Hovey, was a spur to good. Its presence brought out the noblest qualities in man: heroism, sacrifice, idealism, and brotherhood. People could conquer evil, but they could do so only if they were energetic and bold. Much of Hovey's poetry reflects the social idealism that was beginning to arise in the 1890's, and which would culminate in the liberal movement of the early decades of the twentieth century.

The several different movements—nationalism, agrarianism, urban reform—had a common purpose: to extend the promises of American life to large numbers of the population who were being denied them. Reformers and philanthropists, such as Jacob Riis and Jane Addams, looked for methods to improve life in the slums. Farmers organized to thwart exploitation by railroads and money lenders. Laborers too fought for better working conditions and job security, and they carried their cause to open conflict in the Homestead and Pullman strikes. Walter Rauschenbush, a young minister to the working classes in New York, began to formulate the principles of his "Social Gospel." Journalists wrote muckraking articles exposing monopolies and trusts; novelists turned from Romance to fiction with a purpose. Almost anyone could find a reform movement to be associated with: conservation, women's rights, child labor, temperance. This entire progressive movement was probably best expressed in the speeches and writings of that rising young New York politician—Theodore Roosevelt.

Roosevelt pointed out that virtue did not exist in a negative way, nor was it found in a withdrawn life. True virtue required vigor, courage, and common sense. Like Emerson before him, he praised the doer, the man of action. He called for the wealthy young men of the nation to follow him into politics, to act and not to sit back and criticize. He asked for them to give up "ignoble ease" and to live "the strenuous life," the life of action and conflict; to be unselfish and heroic; and to avoid "scrambling materialism."[20] These ideas are similar to Hovey's.

One heroic course of action, argued Roosevelt, was participation in a war fought for humanitarian reasons; for there were times when peace could be more ignoble than war. Hovey voiced the same idea on several occasions in his Arthurian plays, such as *The Marriage of Guenevere*. War brought out the glorious and noble; it reinforced comradeship. In peace, men grew more selfish and competitive; they followed their petty ends and wallowed in avarice. War, then, was an opportunity for men to leave their "scrambling materialism" and to exercise the higher virtues. War could also help unite a people, as Hovey's Arthur indicates:

> You, Merlin, know full well
> The unity of Britain is the heart
> And purpose of my life; but I conceive
> This war will make the country more at one
> Than all our statecraft, for old enmities
> Will melt away into one common heart
> When Britons fight against a common foe.[21]

The Spanish-American War was a conflict tailor-made for the thinking of both Roosevelt and Hovey. Here was a war that could be fought on humanitarian grounds: to free a brave but helpless Cuba that was being oppressed and exploited by an Old World monarchy. Here was an opportunity for triumphant democracy to assert itself and for evil to be eliminated. Moreover, this war of liberation would bring the people of America closer together and help heal the still smarting wounds from the Civil War. Roosevelt's contribution is well known; Hovey's is also significant.

Immediately after the battleship "Maine" was blown up in February, 1898, Hovey responded with "The Word of the Lord from Havana." This poem, written in the diction and cadence of the Bible, is an angry Lord speaking. The people of America, who have become selfish and callous, ignore the cries of the oppressed. America, the mother of revolution, has forgotten her responsibility to those who are trying to remove the yoke of imperialism. The sinking of the "Maine" was the word of the Lord to remind America of its responsibility, and Americans should remember the "Maine" as they did the Alamo. Although the phrase, "Remember the 'Maine'," probably occurred to thousands at the same time, Hovey was one of the first to put it into writing and perhaps the only one to work it into some form of literature.

The Spanish-American War satisfied all the romantic desires of Richard Hovey and his fellow Americans. Here was an opportunity to shove aside the sordidness of trade and to search for high adventure. Cuba became the fair lady in distress, locked in the turret of a castle, held prisoner by a wicked duke. It was the old plot of romance, the theme of melodrama, the subject of best-selling novels, such as G. B. McCutcheon's *Graustark*. There was a new world waiting to be born—a world of hope and freedom that was being held back by decayed aristocracies and materialistic interests—and the clear-eyed Connecticut Yankee would set things right. If Hovey had any doubts about the righteousness of America's cause, all he needed to do was watch the stock market go down with every news release about the war; for anything that hurt Wall Street had to be good.

Hovey put most of his thinking about the war into a long poem, "The Call of the Bugles," that was read before a Grand Army of the Republic gathering on Memorial Day, 1898. He began with a salute to veterans of America's past wars, recalling the taps played less than two years before at his father's funeral in Arlington. Now the country was drawing strength for the conflict at hand from this reservoir of past heroic energy. The real enemy was not so much

Spain as it was financial imperialism, the monopolies in America and those European nations who engaged in geopolitics only out of self-interest. But America was above that, Hovey believed; it had a mission and purpose to protect the weak from the strong. War was not only necessary; it was right.

The belligerency of Hovey's poetry is probably a good index to the passion that most Americans felt during the war. Although there were some critics of America's drift toward imperialism, there were many who desired an increased participation in international affairs. There were those who wished more trade, and allied with them was the American Navy which wanted a chain of coaling stations around the world. Then there were the "jingoes" who out of a surfeit of national pride wanted to extend American sovereignty. Samoa had come under the flag, and Hawaii and the Spanish possessions could also be added. The cry of "manifest destiny" that had pushed the States to the Pacific Ocean was heard once more, and the argument was revived that America's duty was to extend the benefit of democratic institutions to the world.

Hovey agreed with this viewpoint to an extent, but he had even larger hopes for his country's mission. In the poem with the ironic title, "Unmanifest Destiny," which is by far the best of the war pieces, he points out that America's opportunity is boundless and unlimited:

> To what new fates, my country, far
>   And unforeseen of foe or friend,
> Beneath what unexpected star,
>   Compelled to what unchosen end.
>
> Across the sea that knows no beach
>   The Admiral of Nations guides
> Thy blind obedient keels to reach
>   The harbor where thy future rides!
>
> The guns that spoke at Lexington
>   Knew not that God was planning then
> The trumpet word of Jefferson
>   To bugle forth the rights of men.
>
>   . . .
>
> There is a Hand that bends our deeds
>   To mightier issues than we planned,
> Each son that triumphs, each that bleeds,
>   My country, serves Its dark command.

> I do not know beneath what sky
>   Nor on what seas shall be thy fate;
> I only know it shall be high,
>   I only know it shall be great.[22]

Hovey actually seems to have been disappointed by the peace treaty. America had much work to do; not until the world was secure under Anglo-Saxon law could there be real peace with men united in brotherhood. For the battle abroad was the same as the old cause at home: the bringing in of the New World that contained promise, freedom, and plenty for everyone.

Hovey's rather bland college-boy Socialism was not a foreign import but a native product. He was not a disciple of Karl Marx but of Henry George, the San Francisco printer, whose *Progress and Poverty* had become the working man's Bible. George asked why poverty should be increasing at the same time that society was making such great material progress through inventions and technology. He traced the origin of modern economic evils to the ownership of land, and he proposed a single tax upon this source of aristocratic wealth. Although George's agrarian economics were hardly applicable for a country that was rapidly turning industrial, it made sense to his readers who were Western farmers whose grain was used to pay the interest on a mortgage held by an Eastern bank or who were steel workers and miners who lived in company-owned shacks and bought groceries at company stores. More important was his idea that capital and wages were not inversely related but that capital could increase as wages did.

George's book was more influential as a protest than as a plan, and it became one of the intellectual bases for the revolutionary spirit of the 1890's. However, by the time of George's death in 1897 the force of the revolt was weakening. The return of prosperity after the panic of 1893 and legislative adoption of some of the reforms helped ease the dissent. Hovey, in a brief elegy to George, called for the revolution to continue: George's death should signal a beginning and not an end. Even if the reformers had lost the day, the battle was still to continue.[23]

Richard Hovey was basically a radical at heart in politics, in poetics, even in such small matters as dress and behavior. Whether he inherited his radicalism or acquired it from the environment cannot be determined. Personality is a complex of genetic and acquired traits, a blend of nature and nurture. There does seem to be a heredity factor in the trait for independence, and the social conditions of a certain time and place can develop this independence into radicalism. Hovey lived and worked in a time of oppressing conformity; yet it was also a time when an old order was dying and a new one was struggling to be born. Had Richard Hovey lived into the first decades of the twentieth century, he probably would have become a Progressive, a Bull Mooser behind Teddy Roosevelt. But the twentieth century, which would realize so many of Hovey's hopes and deny so many others, was denied him. He died on February 24, 1900, when he was only thirty-five—in the middle of his life.

CHAPTER 2

Songs from Vagabondia

T HE cover of the 1894 edition of *Songs from Vagabondia* has an illustration by Tom Meteyard that is a disc portrait of the three comrades; and Bliss Carman's blond head is between the bearded and swarthy features of Meteyard and Hovey. The front endpaper contains a design of masted sailing ships at a wharf, and the rear paper has a drawing of tall pines along the sea. The mood, one of both adventure and reflection, matches well the cumulative effect of the poems. The slim, tan volume begins with Hovey's "Vagabondia," an expansion of one of Hovey's undergraduate efforts. Like many a college poem, it loudly praises freedom and liberty. The freedom is not desired just for itself or for the sake of license but for those more worthwhile values, Art and Letters, and for the pleasures of creation symbolized by music and wine, Myrtle and Wanda. These are the true riches, but they can be achieved only when the spirit is liberated.

Perhaps even more important is the poetic freedom of the poem itself. The rhymes are not forced into any regular mold: there are couplets, alternating and interlocking rhymes. Hovey also used assonance and repeated words, and sometimes a sound is left dangling with no completing rhyme at all. Anapestic and iambic rhythms are mixed in short lines which range from four to six syllables. But Hovey's metrical arrangement is spontaneous and free since he wrote no set pattern of four-, five-, or six- syllable lines. Form follows function, and the length of the line is adjusted to fit the sentiment of the moment.

It has been said that modern American verse is a blend of Walt Whitman and Emily Dickinson. Whitman's line was long and uneven; Dickinson's, short and regular. Twentieth-century poets have favored the short but uneven line, and Stephen Crane has generally been given credit for making the combination. But Hovey certainly did it earlier because "Vagabondia," or at least part of it, was written when he was still a student at Dartmouth. Anyway, the poem has a certain freshness and a vitality that make it distinct from most nineteenth-century verse.

The poem does have a certain relevance. It could have appeared in a high school or undergraduate literary magazine during the 1960's.

> What have we
> To do with the way
> Of the Pharisee?
> We go or we stay
> At our own sweet will;
> We think as we say,
> And we say or keep still
> At our own sweet will,
> At our own sweet will.
> Here we are free
> To be good or bad,
> Sane or mad,
> Merry or grim
> As the mood may be,—
> Free as the whim
> Of a spook on a spree,—
> Free to be oddities.
> Not mere commodities,
> Stupid and salable,
> Wholly available,
> Ranged upon shelves;
> Each with his puny form
> In the same uniform,
> Cramped and disabled;
> We are not labelled,
> We are ourselves.[1]

I *The Passive Life*

One thought broached in *Vagabondia* is that the really worthwhile life is not found in the bustle of the market place but off to the side, "Like a throstle/ A-joy in the bush." This dominant theme of Hovey's is perhaps best stated in "The Faun," a long reflective poem that is interesting for its liberated meter, its varied rhyme scheme, and its syncopated rhythms. The poet identifies with a faun, the mythical creature that served as a link between man and nature; and the Classical allusions seem to indicate that the truths discovered in nature are eternal. Nebuchadnezzar, whom society thought mad, was really closer to truth than most men; for he considered it necessary to free oneself from custom and convention because only in freedom could one achieve the highest values and the greatest joy:

> I will go out to grass with that old King,
> For I am weary of clothes and cooks.
> I long to lie along the banks of brooks,
> And watch the boughs above me sway and swing.
> Come, I will pluck off custom's livery,
> Nor longer be a lackey to old Time.
> Time shall serve me, and at my feet shall fling
> The spoil of listless minutes. I shall climb
> The wild trees for my food, and run
> Through dale and upland as a fox runs free,
> Laugh for cool joy and sleep i' the warm sun,
> And men will call me mad, like that old King. . . . [2]

The idea that truth can be achieved only by renouncing the sort of life that most men consider worthwhile is implicit in several other Hovey poems. In "Launa Dee," a vagabond love lyric, the protagonist tells his love that he is weary of the vanity, ambition, and struggle that make up life. All things will eventually decay, and it would be better for the two of them to live closely wrapped in dreams. The primitive desires inherited from some mysterious past are better guides to ultimate values than the calculating reasons of modern life. In fact, animals seem to possess a wisdom greater than man's:

> I am sure the snarling
> Beasts could never bungle
> Life as men do, darling,
> Who half know.[3]

"Evening on the Potomac" is an Impressionistic poem in which Hovey is concerned first with creating an effect—that of beauty. The time is a May evening when the air is fragrant and sweet from the Southern spring. The poet, or whoever receives the impression, is on a hilltop overlooking the river and the city of Washington, D.C.

He sees the city as a beautiful girl, an object of desire; and the poem is, therefore, about a young man's ambition. Glory awaits him, but he is not seeking it like a rapacious conquistador or whimpering for it like a child. Instead, his attitude is similar to that of John Keats in his "Two Sonnets on Fame"; he is going to play hide-and-seek and let the glory come to him:

> The fervid breath of our flushed Southern May
> Is sweet upon the city's throat and lips,
> As a lover's whose tired arm slips
> Listlessly over the shoulder of a queen.
>
> Far away
> The river melts in the unseen.
> Oh, beautiful Girl-City, how she dips
> Her feet in the stream
> With a touch that is half a kiss and half a dream!
> Her face is very fair,
> With flowers for smiles and sunlight in her hair.
>
> My westland flower-town, how serene she is!
> Here on this hill from which I look at her,
> All is still as if a worshipper
> Left at some shrine his offering.
>
> Soft winds kiss
> My cheek with a slow lingering.
> A luring whisper where the laurels stir
> Wiles my heart back to woodland-ward again.
>
> But lo,
> Across the sky the sunset couriers run,
> And I remain
> To watch the imperial pageant of the Sun
> Mock me, an impotent Cortez here below,
> With splendors of its vaster Mexico.
>
> O Eldorado of the templed clouds!
> O golden city of the western sky!
> Not like the Spaniard would I storm thy gates;
> Not like the babe stretch chubby hands and cry
> To have thee for a toy; but far from crowds,
> Like my Faun brother in the ferny glen,
> Peer from the wood's edge while thy glory waits,
> And in the darkening thickets plunge again.[4]

II *The Strenuous Life*

Most of Hovey's lyrics are not so drowsy or so quiet as "Evening on the Potomac"; for most of them praise the life of adventure and daring led by the roving, restless spirit; and the rhythm and meter of these poems are as energetic as the message. For Hovey did not regard all ambition or action as bad; only that which was directed toward worldly values or sham goals was so considered. The sort of action that merely imitates others is wasted energy, but action directed toward spiritual and independent goals is real and satisfying. This type of quest is found in "The Wander-Lovers," a poem written while Hovey was camping in Nova Scotia with Mrs. Russell. In the early stanzas, "Marna" is pictured as the ideal companion, roaming the wide world, free and gay. But, as the poem progresses, she becomes more of a representation of man's restless spirit. She has many qualities of nature: her eyes are "sky-blue"; her heart is like an aspen with its "sudden quivers"; her will is like the wind; she is the child of both fire and sea. Artless, dauntless, and very hopeful, Marna is really a symbol for man's spiritual powers—of his bold imagination and his aspiration for the highest good:

> Down the world with Marna!
> That's the life for me!
> Wandering with the wandering wind,
> Vagabond and unconfined!
> Roving with the roving rain
> Its unboundaried domain!
> Kith and kin of wander-kind,
> Children of the sea!
>
> .   .   .
>
> Down the world with Marna,
> Daughter of the fire!
> Marna of the deathless hope,
> Still alert to win new scope
> Where the wings of life may spread
> For a flight unhazarded!
> Dreaming of the speech to cope
> With the heart's desire!
>
> Marna of the far quest
> After the divine!
> Striving ever for some goal
> Past the blunder-God's control!

> Dreaming of potential years
> When no day shall dawn in fears!
> That's the Marna of my soul,
> Wander-bride of mine![5]

The theme of searching is continued in "Discovery," which is an imitation of Rudyard Kipling. Hovey used an eight-line stanza, alternating four-stress and three-stress lines. The rhythm is a mixture of anapest and iambic that provides a quick, skipping movement. But the poem is most notable for its rhyme scheme with which Hovey even surpasses Kipling. Each long line rhymes internally, the rhyme falls on the second and fourth stressed syllables, and the shorter lines rhyme with each other. The action and feeling are somewhat similar to Joseph Conrad's *Youth*. A ship is sailing through uncharted seas, and the crew does not know what it will find. The men feel that they are near land as the sun sets; and, as they wait through the night, they wonder what the morning will bring. The poem is obviously about the excitement of discovery, for the unknown lands could be anything new: new knowledge, new experiences, new feelings.

> When the bugler morn shall wind his horn,
> And we wake to the wild to be,
> Shall we open our eyes on the selfsame skies
> And stare at the selfsame sea?
> O new, new day! though you bring no stay
> To the strain of the sameness grim,
> You are new, new, new—new through and through,
> And strange as a lawless dream.
>
> Will the driftwood float by the lonely boat
> And our prisoner hearts unbar,
> As it tells of the strand of an unseen land
> That lies not far, not far?
> O new, new hope! O sweep and scope
> Of the glad, unlying sea!
> You are new, new, new—with the promise true
> Of the dreamland isles to be.
>
> Will the land-birds fly across the sky,
> Though the land is not to see?
> Have they dipped and passed in the sea-line vast?
> Have we left the land a-lee?

O new despair! though the hopeless air
Grow foul with the calm and grieves,
You are new, new, new—and we cleave to you
As a soul to its freedom cleaves.

Does the falling night hide fiends to fight
And phantoms to affray?
What demons lurk in the grisly mirk,
As the night-watch waits for day?
O strange new gloom! we await the doom,
And what doom none may deem;
But it's new, new, new—and we'll sail it through,
While the mocking sea-gulls scream

A light, a light, in the dead of night,
That lifts and sinks in the waves!
What folk are they who have kindled its ray,—
Men or the ghouls of graves?
O new, new fear! near, near and near,
And you bear us weal or woe!
But you're new, new, new—so a cheer for you!
And onward—friend or foe!

Shall the lookout call from the foretop tall,
"Land, land!" with a maddened scream,
And the crew in glee from the taffrail see
Where the island palm-trees dream?
New heart, new eyes! For the morning skies
Are a-chant with their green and gold!
New, new, new, new—now through and through!
New, new till the dawn is old![6]

III *Comrades*

It has already been mentioned that the lyric "Comrades," in which Hovey traces comradeship through a progression of drinking, fighting, roaming, and dying, concludes *Songs from Vagabondia*. For both Hovey and Carman, the spiritual qualities realized from comradeship are paramount; and in Hovey's case these values certainly transcend those more commonly associated with respectability. A good deal of masculine comradeship involves drinking, and Hovey wrote many drinking songs, some apparently occasional pieces written at the time of the drinking bout itself. One of his better bacchanalian efforts is "The Kavanagh" which, despite its Scottish setting, is not about a gathering of the clan:

> A stone jug and a pewter mug,
> And a table set for three!
> A jug and a mug at every place,
> And a biscuit or two with Brie!
> Three stone jugs of Cruiskeen Lawn,
> And a cheese like crusted foam!
> The Kavanagh receives to-night!
> McMurrough is at home![7]

The poem is really about a reunion of three friends who think about a fourth (perhaps Tom Meteyard) who is studying art in Italy. They conclude that their friend would be better off with them tonight, for friendship is more valuable than art. The three at home possess greater treasures than any museum: the moonlight on the floor, their drink, and "three stout hearts to drain."

Vagabonds, living lives that contrast to middle-class convention, feel some kinship with others who dwell outside the pale of philistine morality. In the poem "The Buccaneers," such characters are only a bolder and more daring type of vagabond. Their life is not one of quiet pleasures of hearth and home. Those who live under the protection of the state may enjoy a regulated happiness, but the buccaneers have to take their pleasure when they can, intemperately if they must. The cautious citizen takes no chances; his greatest value is security. The buccaneers, on the other hand, risk everything with each action:

> Oh, not for us the easy mirth
> Of men that never roam!
> The crackling of the narrow hearth,
> The cabined joys of home!
> Keep your tame, regulated glee,
> O pale protected State!
> Our dwelling-place is on the sea,
> Our joy the joy of Fate!
>
> No long caresses give us ease,
> No lazy languors warm;
> We seize our mates as the sea-gulls seize,
> And leave them to the storm.
> But in the bridal halls of gloom
> The couch is stern and strait;
> For us the marriage rite of Doom,
> The nuptial joy of Fate.

Wine for the weaklings of the town,
Their lucky toasts to drain!
Our skoal for them whose star goes down,
Our drink the drink of men!
No Bacchic ivy for our brows!
Like vikings, we await
The grim, ungarlanded carouse
We keep to-night with Fate.

Ho, gamesters of the pampered court!
What stakes are those at strife?
Your thousands are but paltry sport
To them that play for life.
You risk doubloons, and hold your breath,
Win groats, and wax elate;
But we throw loaded dice with Death,
And call the turn on Fate.

The kings of earth are crowned with care.
Their poets wail and sigh;
Our music is to do and dare,
Our empire is to die.
Against the storm we fling our glee
And shout, till Time abate
The exultation of the sea,
The fearful joy of Fate.[8]

The viewpoint of the lawless outsider is found also in "The Outlaw." The speaker is a bandit who is commenting on the pleasures
and comforts enjoyed by the Lord of Jarlwell who has gold, lands,
and many servants. The outlaw has nothing but his cunning and
strength, but he will eventually destroy the lord and take all his
possessions. All the outlaw needs is patience to wait until he can
enjoy the last laugh.

IV Love Songs

Most of Hovey's love lyrics are sentimental pieces; full of melancholy and tender thoughts, they are typical of the love poetry of his
time. Read silently, these lyrics are somewhat ineffective because
there is too much reliance on pathetic fallacy—the woods are always
sad, and the surf always sobs. But, when read aloud, the poems have
more vitality and meaning; and they were probably showpieces for
Hovey's dramatic voice.

Somewhat different from the lyrics described above is "A King's Son," an imitation Scottish ballad that combines several of Hovey's favorite themes: independence, true love, and rejection of commercial considerations. As the mother and daughter are talking in alternative stanzas, the daughter indicates all the several advantages in marrying the king's son; but the mother (certainly not typical of most mothers of that or any time) argues that the daughter would be better off to be an outlaw, a traitor, or a whore than to marry for gold and prestige:

"Daughter, daughter, marry no man,
Though a king's son come to woo,
If he be not more than blessing or ban
To the secret soul of you."

" 'Tis the King's son, indeed, I ween,
And he left me even but now,
And he shall make me a dazzling queen,
With a gold crown on my brow."

"And are you one that a golden crown,
Or the list of a name can lure?
You had better wed with a country clown,
And keep your young heart pure."

"Mother, the King has sworn, and said
That his son shall wed but me;
And I must gang to the prince's bed,
Or a traitor I shall be."

"Oh, what care you for an old man's wrath?
Or what care you for a king?
I had rather you fled on an outlaw's path,
A rebel, a hunted thing."

"Mother, it is my father's will,
For the King has promised him fair
A goodly earldom of hollow and hill,
And a coronet to wear."

"Then woe is worth a father's name,
For it names your dourest foe!
I had rather you came the child of shame
Than to have you fathered so."

"Mother, I shall have gold enow,
Though love be never mine,
To buy all else that the world can show
Of good and fair and fine."

"Oh, what care you for a prince's gold,
Or the key of a kingdom's till?
I had rather see you a harlot bold
That sins of her own free will.

"For I have been wife for the stomach's sake,
And I know whereof I say;
A harlot is sold for a passing slake,
But a wife is sold for aye.

"Body and soul for a lifetime sell,
And the price of the sale shall be
That you shall be harlot and slave as well
Until Death set you free."[9]

Quite a stylistically different love poem is "At Sea," written in free verse. The experience underlying the poem probably stemmed from Hovey's return voyage from Europe and the separation from Mrs. Russell. The seas are heavy; the night is dark; there are no stars above; and the only light is a beacon far astern. But the steamer forges ahead like a brave man going to his destiny. The poet, sitting along on the fantail in the mist, feels that he is being swept irresistibly and helplessly to his fate. But he does not care; because he is separated from his love, a heavy heartsickness has stripped him of hope. The poem seems to be saying that people are mentally alive only when in love or near their loves. Love, for Hovey, was far more important than a means for providing sexual satisfaction or security; to him, love was the generating power of the spirit and the imagination. To be alive, to be creative, a person had to be in love.

As a brave man faces the foe,
Alone against hundreds, and sees Death grin in his teeth,
But, shutting his lips, fights on to the end
Without speech, without hope, without flinching,—
So, silently, grimly, the steamer
Lurches ahead through the night.

A beacon-light far off,
Twinkling across the waves like a star!

But no star in the dark overhead!
The splash of waters at the prow, and the evil light
Of the death-fires flitting like will-o'-the-wisps beneath!
  And beyond
Silence and night!

I sit by the taffrail,
Alone in the dark and the blown cold mist and the spray,
Feeling myself swept on irresistibily,
Sunk in the night and the sea, and made one with their footfall-less onrush.
Letting myself be borne like a spar adrift
Helplessly into the night.

Without fear, without wish,
 Insensate save of a dull, crushed ache in my heart,
Careless whither the steamer is going,
Conscious only as in a dream of the wet and the dark
And of a form that looms and fades indistinctly
Everywhere out of the night.

O love, how came I here?
Shall I wake at thy side and smile at my dream?
The dream that grips me so hard that I cannot wake nor stir!
O love! O my own love, found but to be lost!
My soul sends over the waters a wild inarticulate cry,
Like a gull's scream heard in the night.

The mist creeps closer. The beacon
Vanishes astern. The sea's monotonous noises
Lapse through the drizzle with a listless, subsiding cadence.
And thou, O love, and the sea throb on in my brain together,
While the steamer plunges along,
Butting its way through the night.[10]

Of the thirty-three poems in the first collection of *Vagabondia*,
Hovey contributed nineteen. Although on a scattering of subjects,
they group themselves around several themes. There is the theme
of the inactive spirit, or the spirit held in the suspended animation
necessary to gain real insight into truth. Contrary to this feeling are
the poems like "The Wander-Lovers" and "Discovery" that praise
man's restless spirit as it searches for eternal values. But both with-
drawal and action require courage, and that quality is best derived
from the love of comrades. Underneath all these poems beats the
pulse of *carpe diem*, but the "living today" is for more than just
sensual pleasure. People should direct their lives toward beauty,

truth, and goodness; and, unless they pursue these values in their highest forms, they are being unfaithful to their true selves. However, these values are attainable only in an atmosphere of a freedom that allows each person to develop his own sacred and peculiar identity.

CHAPTER 3

More Songs from Vagabondia

More Songs (1896), the second volume of the vagabond songs, is very similar in design to the first one. Meteyard did change the illustrations: the front inside cover pictures a lazy river, trees, a canoe, and a Huck Finn; and the back paper features hills and groves and poets at work. These artistic impressions, which do not convey the feelings of excitement and adventure that the first volume had, are however, an accurate representation. The poetry is generally more calm and dreamy; there is less vigor and protest. Indeed, *More Songs* definitely lacks the feeling of rollicking protest the earlier volume has. Almost a third larger than the preceding volume, *More Songs* contains fifty-four poems, twenty-eight of them by Hovey. There are pieces written on the occasion of children's birthdays, and there are also eulogies to Robert Browning, Robert Louis Stevenson, Shakespeare, and Paul Verlaine.

One of the subjects of the earlier volume had been the many forms that vagabondage could take. *More Songs* begins with Hovey's rhymed free-verse poem "Jongleurs" in which the vagabonds have become like those wandering minstrels who used to entertain Medieval villages with song and story. The poem starts with the excitement felt as the Jongleurs arrive. The villagers have been striving against one another, "Fighting for leeway for laughter,/ Toiling for leisure for loving!"[1] Now they give up their several pursuits—lay down ledgers, picks and shovels, "Deals, over-reachings,/ Worries and griefs,/ Teachings and preachings"—and go to the street corner where the Jongleurs are.

Who are these wandering, entertaining people in garb both tattered and sumptuous? Where have they come from, and where will they go? Someone has heard that they have come from the moon; they have seen Eldorado; they have been in Lebanon and Ophir and played for the Khan in Tartary. Their song is a "lyric experiment" that rises like a lark out of the maze of thought "to the blue sky of wonder." The music continually changes: it goes from a lover's song to the "lilt of a loafer." The sounds of heaven mingle with the sounds of earth; the songs of Nature blend with the song of man. As the villagers feel their spirits rise with the music, they become freer, braver, and more united in brotherhood:

> How our feet itch to keep time to their measure!
> How our hearts lift to the lilt of their song!
> Let the world go, for a day's royal pleasure!
> Not every summer such waifs come along.

When the performance is over, the Jongleurs go to the inn. They drink and laugh, but their merriment is always clean: "Gentlemen even in jollity—/ Certainly people of quality." Although they are homeless and penniless and are just wayside strummers going from town to town, they know how to live. They are spendthrifts of life; but, the more of their days they enjoy, the greater their supply of time becomes:

> For joy and love and vision
> Are alive and breed and stay
> When dust shall hold in derision
> The misers of a day.

The Jongleurs have discovered the secret of immortality: they concentrate upon values and activities that are permanent. They lay up their treasures in heaven.

I *Contentment*

The perplexing difficulty about these permanent values is that they cannot be aggressively sought like the values of wealth, fame, and power. They are more states of mind than commodities, and any aggression could destroy the mental equipoise necessary to receive them. Indeed, these prizes could come unsolicited when a person hides faun-like in the thick of the forest. In "The Wood-God," the poet, who had admitted that he was half faun, seeks his ancient brother. But his search is in vain since, wherever he goes, he hears parting footsteps. When he leaves the trail and lies on the moss, he lets the garter snake crawl across his neck, and he minds neither the clouds nor leaves that float above. His mind becomes a blank, a transparent eyeball; and the wood god that he has been pursuing appears suddenly at his side. Only by surrendering himself completely to Nature and by losing his individuality does he receive those values which Nature symbolizes. The same lesson is learned by Isaac McCaslin in Faulkner's *The Bear:* Ike has to yield himself completely to Nature—give up his gun and compass before he can see Old Ben.

This theme about passive acceptance is continued in several other lyrics, such as "A Faun's Song," which utilizes repetition, rhyme, and sound to achieve a passive effect:

> Cool! Cool! Cool!
> Cool and sweet
> The feel of the moss at my feet!
> And sweet and cool
> The touch of the wind, of the wind!
>
> Cool wind out of the blue,
> At the touch of you
> A little wave crinkles and flows
> All over me down to my toes.
>
> "Coo-loo! Coo-loo!"
> Hear the doves in the tree-tops croon.
> "Coo-loo! Coo-loo!"
> Love comes soon.
>
> "June! June!"
> The veery sings,
> Sings and sings,
> "June! June!"
> A pretty tune!
>
> Wind with your weight of perfume,
> Bring me the bluebells' bloom![2]

Fauns and dryads are mythical representations of the woodland spirit, but a more realistic symbol can be found in the birds. In "September Woodlands," the yellowbirds flit about happily, and they are too wise to brood. Their mood is one of contentment and not melancholy. An even better symbol is found in "The Mocking-Bird." American poets, who have frequently despaired because they lacked the nightingale to write about, have never realized the symbolic potential of the mockingbird. This amazing creature, which can imitate some fifty-five different calls, can sing for hours without repeating itself. Its variety and complexity are truly representative of American life, yet few American poets (Whitman is a notable exception) have written about it. For Hovey, the mockingbird's song contains the secret of the fauns and the woods, but the bird chooses not to reveal this secret to man. Actually, doing so would be to no avail since no knowledge or action, except surrender, can lead man to these ultimate truths.

> Hear! hear! hear!
> Listen! the word
> Of the mocking-bird!
> Hear! hear! hear!
> I will make all clear;
> I will let you know
> Where the footfalls go
> That through the thicket and over the hill
> Allure, allure.
> How the bird-voice cleaves
> Through the weft of leaves
> With a leap and a thrill
> Like the flash of a weaver's shuttle, swift and sudden and sure!
>
> And lo, he is gone—even while I turn
> The wisdom of his runes to learn.
> He knows the mystery of the wood,
> The secret of the solitude;
> But he will not tell, he will not tell,
> For all he promises so well.[3]

But birds and animals are not the only creatures who can possess this equanimity and joy. A few humans can too, such as the man who is the subject of "Barney McGee." This poem—one which probably was a standard for elocution classes for several decades because of its daring rhymes, its complex but bouncing rhythms, and its tongue-twisting diction—has to be read aloud to be understood. The poem is the characterization of a happy-go-lucky Irishman, who, according to Carman, was the captain of a ship that sailed from Boston to Nova Scotia.[4] Barney is a high-spirited person, a lover of poetry, drink, and women; and Hovey salutes him as a fellow vagabond. The style of the poem is an attempt to capture in words the joyous character of Barney McGee:

Barney McGee, there's no end of good luck in you,
Will-o'-the-wisp, with a flicker of Puck in you,
Wild as a bull-pup and all of his pluck in you,—
Let a man tread on your coat and he'll see!—
Eyes like the lakes of Killarney for clarity,
Nose that turns up without any vulgarity,
Smile like a cherub and hair that is carroty,—
Wow, you're a rarity, Barney McGee!
Mellow as Tarragon,
Prouder than Aragon—
Hardly a paragon,
You will agree—
Here's all that's fine to you!
Books and old wine to you!
Girls be divine to you,
Barney McGee!. . .[5]

II *On the Road*

The second volume of vagabond verse does have a few songs that celebrate the wanderlust. "Three of a Kind" is an autobiographical poem that relates a hiking excursion Hovey made with Meteyard and Carman along the Maine Coast. The poem contains many sharp images of the New England autumn: the rocky farms and rail fences, the colorful woods, the salt-spray gusts from the ocean, the honking of wild geese, the stinging air, the flocks of crows settling on fallow land. The three comrades are, of course, ragged and hungry but carefree and happy. They hope to continue through life with pure hearts and strong friends.

The "Hunting-Song from 'King Arthur' " also praises the outdoor life and action. Those who love ease and who stay close to hearth and home are strangers to the joys of the open air and to the thrill of danger. Another poem that develops this theme of discovery through effort is "The Sea Gypsy." This short lyric, a classic of vagabond poetry, opens on a note of restlessness:

I am fevered with the sunset,
I am fretful with the bay,
For the wander-thirst is on me
And my soul is in Cathay.

There's a schooner in the offing,
With her topsails shot with fire,

> And my heart has gone aboard her
> For the Islands of Desire.
>
> I must forth again to-morrow!
> With the sunset I must be
> Hull down on the trail of rapture
> In the wonder of the sea.[6]

While this poem no doubt owes something to Kipling's "Mandalay" for setting and to Tennyson's "Ulysses" for imagery and idea, these influences do not lesson its worth. The idea is that aspiration requires daring; without a restlessness of spirit, men would make no advance.

In the ballad "Premonition," which has two lovers parting at night, the man promises that the next morning will find them reunited on a journey toward joy. But, as he walks into the sunset, the woman shudders from an unanticipated fear:

> He said, "Good-night, my heart is light,
> To-morrow morn at day
> We two together in the dew
> Shall forth and fare away.
>
> "We shall go down the halls of dawn
> To find the doors of joy;
> We shall not part again, dear heart."
> And he laughed out like a boy.
>
> He turned and strode down the blue road
> Against the western sky
> Where the last line of sunset glowed
> As sullen embers die.
>
> The night reached out her kraken arms
> To clutch him as he passed,
> And for one sudden moment
> My soul shrank back aghast.[7]

III *The Poet of the Body*

Walt Whitman had advertised himself as the poet of the body as well as of the soul. Taking issue with the Puritan clergy who had seen the body as the residence of man's baser instincts which ought to be repressed or at best only grudgingly satisfied, Whitman considered the body as natural and beautiful and its desires as good things. Hovey also celebrates the body in several poems, and he leaves little doubt about the identity of his inspiration. These poems are almost direct imitations of Whitman's free verse; but, instead of Whitman's long lines that are slow moving and solid, Hovey's free verse is short-lined, lyrical, and usually rhymed.

"In a Silence" praises a woman's body and her frankness and naturalness in love. Specific reference is made to her hair, throat, and lips; there is nothing about physical love to be ashamed of. But true love is more than love of body; it is a matching of souls. This spiritual love, which occurs at the same time as the physical, is the love that will endure. Hovey believed in the ideals of courtly love, as exemplified by Launcelot and Guenevere.

> Heart to heart!
> And the stillness of night and the moonlight, like hushed breathing
> Silently, stealthily moving across thy hair!
>
> O womanly face!
> Tender and strong and lucent with infinite feeling,
> Shrinking with startled joy, like wind-struck water,
> And yet so frank, so unashamed of love!
>
> Ay, for there it is, love—that's the deepest.
> Love's not love in the dark.
> Light loves wither i' the sun, but Love endureth,
> Clothing himself with the light as with a robe.
>
> I would bare my soul to thy sight—
> Leave not a secret deep unsearched,
> Unrevealing its shame or its glory.
> Love without Truth shall die as a soul without God.
> A lying love is the love of a day
> But the brave and true shall love forever.
>
> Build Love a house;
> Let the walls be thick;
> Shut him in from the sight of men;
> But hide not Love from himself.
>
> Ah, the summer night!
> The wind in the trees and the moonlight!
> And my kisses on thy throat
> And thy breathing in my hair!
>
> Silent, lips to lips!
> But our souls have held speech, thought answering echoing thought,
> Though the only words were kisses. [8]

Even more Whitmanesque is Hovey's "The Bather," in which the speaker is a woman who has seen a young man naked. In his body she sees the reflection of the beauties of nature: a heavenly chest and supple limbs. While she knows that women are beautiful, she finds manly physical strength even more beautiful:

> I saw him go down to the water to bathe;
> He stood naked upon the bank.
>
> His breast was like a white cloud in the heaven, that catches the sun;
> It swelled with the sharp joy of the air.
>
> His legs rose with the spring and curve of young birches;
> The hollow of his back caught the blue shadows:
> With his head thrown up to the lips of the wind;
> And the curls of his forehead astir with the wind.
>
> I would that I were a man, they are so beautiful;
> Their bodies are like the bows of the Indians;
> They have the spring and the grace of bows of hickory.
>
> I know that women are beautiful, and that I am beautiful;
> But the beauty of a man is so lithe and alive and triumphant,
> Swift as the flight of a swallow and sure as the pounce of the eagle.[9]

Another poem about the human body is "Shakespeare Himself: for the Unveiling of Mr. Partridge's Statue of the Poet." The American sculptor, William Ordway Partridge, had been commissioned to create a statue of the bard for Lincoln Park in Chicago. Hovey begins by claiming that the body is not the prison house that separates man's soul from its true inheritance, as theologians and poets have so often claimed. Rather, the opposite is true; the body is the means by which man can realize his aspirations. Without the body, so frequently despised, no light would reach the brain, no pleasurable sensation would stir the blood, and no love of nature or mankind would exist. Whatever freedom man has, he finds through the body, not separated from it. In fact, the soul is revealed by the body; and the sculptor, with his art, attempts to portray the spiritual quality of man.

Hovey then turns to the subject at hand and asks that the sculptor mold Shakespeare in the form known by his comrades Ben Jonson and "all the rout" that had gathered for "wit and wine and fellowship" in the taproom of the Mermaid Tavern. He asks the sculptor to

create the face that charmed his comrades so; to carve the grace that
captured Ann Hathaway; to form the hand that clasped first the Earl
of Southampton's and then the "dark lady" of the sonnets; to mold
the eyes that wept when his son Hamnet died; and to carve the lips
that learned from Christopher Marlowe and then taught John
Fletcher and other poets. He wants the sculptor to capture the calm
and serene demeanor of the Shakespeare who retired as a country
squire in Stratford and who looked upon his work and knew it was
good.

The artist should create no idealized Shakespeare but the very
form in which he lived. God is most godlike not when He is the aloof
lawgiver thundering from Mt. Sinai, but when He is like a
companion—when His thoughts match man's. Men are most like
God when they are brought near to their fellow men. Hovey asks
the sculptor to bring Shakespeare near to men—that gentle soul
who made men suffer with his tragic heroines and laugh with
Falstaff. Although Shakespeare must have had a great heart to
create so many characters, he, himself, must have been greater than
any of them. He could not have had the flaws of Othello or Brutus;
his wisdom must have been greater than Hamlet's questions; his
mirth sweeter than Benedick's; his dignity surpassed that of all his
kings; and his enchantment was more magic than Prospero's.
Through these phantom heroes, readers approach the man who
created them: the master poet of all ages whose spirit is ineffable.
Here, where words end, the sculptor's art begins; and men can see
Shakespeare's character now and recognize him as a comrade and a
man.

IV *Nocturnes*

Three poems in *More Songs* show the influence of the Symbolists
upon Hovey. These are nocturnes (night is a favorite Symbolist
backdrop), two of which are appropriately set in France. "Nocturne:
In Anjou" is an unrhymed sonnet, apparently about poetry:

> I dreamed of Sappho on a summer night,
> Her nightingales were singing in the trees
> Beside the castled river; and the wind
> Fell like a woman's fingers on my cheek.
> And then I slept and dreamed and marked no change;
> The night went on with me into my dream.
> This only I remember, that I cried:

"O Sappho! ere I leave this paradise,
Sing me one song of those lost books of yours
For which we poets still go sorrowing;
That when I meet my fellows on the earth
I may rejoice them more than many pearls;"
And she, the sweetly smiling, answered me,
As one who dreams, "I have forgotten them."[10]

In this poem Hovey seems more interested in creating an effect than in developing a thought. The fact that Sappho has forgotten her songs might mean that even poetry has a mortality when compared with nature.

In "Nocturne: In Provence," the other poem redolent with night imagery, soft warm air and moonlight filter into the room along with the song of nightingales. The poet sees his loved one standing naked before him, and she is so tall and beautiful that she is like a creature from another world—more like air and music than body:

The blue night, like an angel, came into the room,—
Came through the open window from the silent sky
Down trellised stairs of moonlight into the dear room
As if a whisper breathed of some divine one nigh.
The nightingales, like brooks of song in Paradise,
Gurgled their serene rapture to the silent sky—
Like springs of laughter bubbling up in Paradise,
The serene nightingales along the riverside
Purled low in every tree their star-cool melodies
Of joy—in every tree along the riverside.

Did the vain garments melt in music from your side?
Did you rise from them as a lily flowers i' the air?
—But you were there before me like the Night's own bride—
I dared not call you mine. So still and tall you were,
I never dreamed that you were mine—I never dreamed
I loved you—I forgot I loved you. You were air
And music, and the shadows that you stood in, seemed
Like priests that keep their sombre vigil round a shrine—
Like sombre priests that watch about a glorious shrine.

And then you stepped into the moonlight and laid bare
The wonder of your body to the night, and stood
With all the stars of heaven looking at you there,
As simply as a saint might bare her soul to God—
As simply as a saint might bathe in lakes of prayer—

> Stood with the holy moonlight falling on you there
> Until I thought that in a glory unaware
> I had seen a soul stand forth and bare itself to God—
> A saintly soul lay bare its innocence to God.[11]

This poem is, first of all, of course, a love poem; but it is also a poem about symbolism. The reality of the room and the body are juxtaposed with the unreal elements: the moonlight, the night air, and nightingale's song. The "blue light" enters the room "like an angel" down the stairsteps of moonlight while the chorus of nightingales sanctify the place. The song and the light melt the garments from the loved one's frame, and the religious motif is developed by the comparison of her naked body to a shrine. When she steps into the moonlight, the body dissolves; and the soul stands forth, baring itself to God. The moonlight and the nightingales are agents that reveal the ideal behind the real. The body is the temple of the spirit.

The third nocturne, "June Night in Washington," is one of the best poems Hovey wrote and is worthy of extended analysis. In this poem, he is not inhibited by rhyme; and he allows himself complete freedom of rhythm and meter: the lines vary in length from four syllables to sixteen. The poem is a happy blend of image and theme, sensation and thought. The parts of the poem help advance the whole, yet the meaning is entirely hidden until the last line. This line is so startling and so unexpected that it arouses the reader's whole stock of sensibilities; he has to think back over the entire poem and then read it again before its meaning begins to be clear to him. And it is the sort of poem he relishes reading again. In this respect, "June Night" is a masterpiece of design for communicating a poetic feeling.

The poem begins with simple imagery, the smell of flowers, the sounds of a summer's eve, the tension between light and dark at twilight. When the sun disappears, its memory is kept alive by the moon and the light of the lamp:

> The scent of honeysuckle,
> Drugging the twilight
> With its sweet opiate of lovers' dreams!
> The last red glow of the setting sun
> On the red brick wall
> Of the neighboring house,
> And the scramble of red roses over it!

Slowly, slowly
The night smokes up from the city to the stars,
The faint foreshadowed stars;
The smouldering night
Breathes upward like the breath
Of a woman asleep
With dim breasts rising and falling
And a smile of delicate dreams.

Softly, softly
The wind comes into the garden,
Like a lover that fears lest he waken his love,
And his hands drip with the scent of the roses
And his locks weep with the opiate odor of honeysuckle.
Sighing, sighing
As a lover that yearns for the lips of his love,
In a torment of bliss,
In a passionate dreaming of bliss,
The wind in the trees of the garden!

How intimate are the trees,—
Rustling like the secret darkness of the soul!
How still is the starlight,—
Aloof in the placidity of dream!

Outside the garden
A group of negroes passing in the street
Sing with ripe lush voices,
Sing with voices that swim
Like great slow gliding fishes
Through the scent of the honeysuckle:

My love's waitin',
Waitin' by the river,
Waitin' till I come along!
Wait there, child; I'm comin'.

Jay-bird tol' me,
Tol' me in the mornin',
Tol' me she'd be there tonight.
Wait there, child; I'm comin'.

Waves of dream!
Spell of the summer night!
Will of the grass that stirs in its sleep!
Desire of the honeysuckle!
And further away,

Like the plash of far-off waves in the fluid night,
The negroes, singing:

Whip-po'-will tol' me,
Tol' me in the evenin',
"Down by the bend where the cat-tails grow."
Wait there, child; I'm comin'.

Lo, the moon,
Like a galleon sailing the night;
And the wash of the moonlight over the roofs and the trees!

Oh, my bride,
Come down from yonder lattice where you bide
Like a charmed princess in a Persian song!
I look up at your yellow window-panes
Set in the night with far-off wizardry.
Come down, come down; the night is fain of you,
The garden waits your footstep on its walks.

Lo, the moon,
Like a galleon sailing the night;
And the wash of the moonlight over the red brick wall and the roses!

A gleam of lamplight through an open door!
A footfall like the wind's upon the grass,
A rustle like the wind's among the leaves! . . .
Dim as a dream of pale peach blooms of light,
Blue in the blue soft pallor of the moon,
She comes between the trees as a faint tune
Falls from a flute far off into the night. . . .
So Death might come to one who knew him Love.[12]

The poem is remarkable for its sustained impression. The reader
can smell the growing fragrance of a June night in the scent of
honeysuckle and roses, feel the soft warm breeze, hear the wind
rustle in the growing grass and heavy-leafed trees, and see the
moonlight bathing the scene. The simple song of the Negroes about
love waiting by the river underlines the theme. The desire of the
lover in the garden for his loved one above him is both natural and
romantic, and so is the loved one's approach. Then, the incongruity
of the last line: "So Death might come to one who knew him Love."
The thought is quite ironic: that amidst all this beauty and growing
fertility and love, Death should enter.

But even though the last line shifts into a different key, from life
to death, the poem does not end on a jarring note. The reader has

been partially conditioned for it by the images and similes of sleep throughout. The night is compared to a sleeping woman, and the wind rises softly like a lover fearful of waking his love. The entire environment is sleep inducing, and a heavy sleep at that. The honeysuckle is called an opiate. Within the sleep, there is a dream, and the dream, induced by the honeysuckle and environment, is one of sensual desire.

The imagery of the earth is dark and dusky; the heavens are the source of light. As the night rises from the city like smoke, the sky retains the rays of the setting sun. The faint stars appear and then the moon, which illumines everything. Finally, the light of the lamp of the loved one appears high above him in a window, and the lover entreats her to come down. The first time the light appears on the ground level occurs when she comes bearing the lamp through the open door. The lover is finally united with something he has long desired—with something that has come from above.

Death might also come like this loved one—beautiful, silent, heaven sent. In "Seaward," (1893) Hovey had praised death as that which releases man to immortality. But Hovey is not writing in "June Night" about physical death, coffins, and tall candles; in this poem death is more an abstraction for self-denial. To love completely, the lover has abandoned his aggressiveness and selfish interests; he must willingly sacrifice his individuality for the benefit of the lover. Therefore, in his desire for Love, he has also unconsciously desired the destruction of himself. This desire is Death, but it is not to be feared. Death enters into life like light into darkness.

The poem offers a good example of the symbolic technique; the imagery is not there just for decoration, for it produces effects and also embodies underlying meaning. The lush fertility of summer, the honeysuckle, and the Negroes' song advance the theme of desire. The "aloof" stars, the moon, and the lamp-lit window represent the aspiration—the thing desired that is something of spiritual and unearthly value. Where earth and heaven come together is that infinite point where parallel lines meet. Love and Death are one.

V *Poetry*

Although Hovey was influenced by the French Symbolists, he was still critical of their pessimism and dissipation. Shortly after Paul Verlaine's death in 1896, Hovey wrote a sonnet to be included in a memorial volume in which he praises the idea of Verlaine's

vagabondage and revolt but asserts that his protest had been too
wild and senseless. Verlaine was caught in chains, and he destroyed
himself trying to break free. This judgment of the cautious American
vagabond Hovey of the more prodigal European implies that protest
and revolt are all right but that they ought to be sensible. Yet
underneath Verlaine's revolt there was purity and benediction—"A
stretch of God's blue calm." As a result, he would surely receive this
calmness now in death.

> Avid of life and love, insatiate vagabond,
> With quest too furious for the graal he would have won,
> He flung himself at the eternal sky, as one
> Wrenching his chains but impotent to burst the bond.
>
> Yet under the revolt, the revel, the despond,
> What pools of innocence, what crystal benison!
> As through a riven mist that glowers in the sun,
> A stretch of God's blue calm glassed in a virgin pond.
>
> Prowler of obscene streets that riot reels along,
> And aisles with incense numb and gardens mad with rose,
> Monastic cells and dreams of dim brocaded lawns,
>
> Death, which has set the calm of Time upon his song,
> Surely upon his soul has kissed the same repose
> In some fair heaven the Christ has set apart for Fauns.[13]

Hovey leaves no doubt, though, that the poetry is achieved only
through emotion and feeling and not through just thought and intellect. In the short poem "Distillation," he compares those who
walk a straight line with the divine, drunken madness of the poet:

> They that eat the uncrushed grape
> Walk with steady heels:
> Lo, now, how they stare and gape
> Where the poet reels!
> He has drunk the sheer divine
> Concentration of the vine.[14]

And why should man try to walk a steady line when much of what is
valuable in art is often accomplished by some mysterious workings
of the imagination. Freud had not yet discovered the libidinal
energy of the subconscious mind, a creative fount that men still

know little of. Before Freud, poets and artists considered the source
to be divine inspiration. Hovey, more humbly, calls it an "Accident
in Art."

> What painter has not with a careless smutch
> Accomplished his despair?—one touch revealing
> All he had put of life, thought, vigor, feeling,
> Into the canvas that without that touch
> Showed of his love and labor just so much
> Raw pigment, scarce a scrap of soul concealing!
> What poet has not found his spirit kneeling
> A-sudden at the sound of such or such
> Strange verses staring from his manuscript,
> Written he knows not how, but which will sound
> Like trumpets down the years? So Accident
> Itself unmasks the likeness of Intent,
> And ever in blind Chance's darkest crypt
> The shrine-lamp of God's purposing is found.[15]

  More Songs concludes, in a manner similar to the first collection,
with one of Hovey's typical lyrics, "At the End of the Day." In this
song, which is another eulogy to comradeship and courage, a small
group of men are trapped and will have to fight the next day against
a large army. The poem could represent the plight of the artist in a
materialistic society, but most readers prefer to find in it the spirit of
brave men who have the courage anywhere and anytime to die
fighting for their beliefs. Such a stand is real immortality.

> There is no escape by the river,
> There is no flight left by the fen;
> We are compassed about by the shiver
> Of the night of their marching men.
> Give a cheer!
> For our hearts shall not give way.
> Here's to a dark to-morrow,
> And here's to a brave today!
>
> The tale of their hosts is countless,
> And the tale of ours a score;
> But the palm is naught to the dauntless,
> And the cause is more and more.
> Give a cheer!
> We may die, but not give way.

Here's to a silent morrow,
And here's to a stout today!

God has said: "Ye shall fail and perish;
But the thrill ye have felt to-night
I shall keep in my heart and cherish
When the worlds have passed in night."
Give a cheer!
For the soul shall not give way.
Here's to the greater to-morrow
That is born of a great today!

Now shame on the craven truckler
And the puling things that mope!
We've a rapture for our buckler
That outwears the wings of hope.
Give a cheer!
For our joy shall not give way.
Here's in the teeth of to-morrow
To the glory of to-day![16]

CHAPTER 4

Launcelot and Guenevere

A schema written by Hovey in 1898 reveals the over-all organization of *Launcelot and Guenevere: A Poem in Dramas*. The design was similar to that of Greek tragedy. There were to be three parts, and each part would consist of three plays. The first play of each part was to be a masque, or a musical drama, "foreshadowing the events to follow, dealing with the supernatural elements of the myth and symbolizing the philosophic, aesthetic and ethical elements of the series."[1] The second play in each series was to be a tragedy, and the third a romantic or idyllic drama. Hovey also distinguished the parts by their subject matter. Part I was concerned with the rising power of the Round Table, Arthur's ambition, and his defeat of Rome. Part II was to present Arthur and the Round Table at their highest power and provide the first mutterings of the fall; and the great event of this part was to be the search for the Holy Grail (which Hovey spelled "Graal"). Part III was to deal with the fall of Arthur and his knights.

I *Merlin: Vision of Fate*

The Quest of Merlin, the masque that introduces Part I, suggests the philosophical drift of the entire poem; and Hovey called it "The Masque of Fate and Evolution."[2] He includes about every minor deity ever mentioned in mythology, beginning with the Norns, the Teutonic goddesses of Fate. There is Argente (the Lady of the Lake and Queen of Avalon), as well as Nimue (the water goddess) and eight other maidens. There are assorted sylphs, gnomes, naiads, and dryads. Pan and Bacchus with their companies of fauns, satyrs, maenads, and bassarids romp through the scenes, together with half the company from *A Midsummer-Night's Dream* (Puck, Oberon, and Titania), plus Ariel from *The Tempest*, and Queen Mab with attendant fairies, elves, and goblins. Aphrodite makes an appearance, as do the loves, the valkyrs, and the angels. In fact, Merlin is the only halfway real person in the piece.

The play chronicles Merlin's progress in his search for knowledge: he goes from the Norns, the finishers of Fate, to the Arcadian deities, and finally to the spirits of Avalon. The opening scenes are largely a collection of songs, which are neither especially distinguished nor helpful in developing the theme. They did provide the young poet an opportunity, however, to experiment with different metrical arrangements. The sylphs' light and airy song, for example, features anapestic rhythms and feminine rhyme:

> There is no one wisteth
> The way that it goeth.
> The wind bloweth
> Whither it listeth,—
> Sweet, sweet.[3]

The gnomes reply to them in heavy truncated lines of trochaic feet and masculine rhyme:

> Under the ground,
> Clogged and bound,
> We strive and strain
> To be rid of the chain,
> As a caged beast rages
> To roam again.

The song of the Naiads, which resolves the two, takes something from both styles:

> Maidenly strong
> With a joyous song,
> Very merry is the river as it ripples along.
> The vales are voicing
> A great rejoicing.[4]

The play does not get down to business until the scene shifts to Avalon, and Merlin meets Argente and Nimue who are the originators of Fate, just as the Norns are its finishers. Merlin explains that his quest is to find the answer to Arthur's desire to marry and produce an heir, and he wonders if Guenevere is the most suitable mate. Nimue conducts Merlin into the Heavens, where the

Angels advise him to close the eyes of the mind and open those of the soul. They inform him that there is a Fate more powerful than the Norns and a Will more primeval than the Origins.

The real truth is that all fates are individual: a man's character is his fate, and his destiny is determined by his temperament. Some are born for glory, others pain:

> And the kingdom of one is joy
> And the kingdom of one is tears;
> One for a dull annoy,
> And one for a sea of cheers!
> Each to his own,
> Whatever the road he take;
> This one to sit on a throne,
> And that one to stand at the stake![5]

So Merlin, good astrologer that he is, will have to look into the heavens for the answer. Arthur's horoscope reveals an imperial character who will have little domestic happiness; for, while his power extends over multitudes, he has little success in dealing with individuals. Launcelot's star is the star of true love, but he has two true loves to satisfy: his comradeship for Arthur and his passion for Guenevere. Guenevere's star has both sovereign and rebellious qualities: she is queenly in manner but not in spirit:

> A bitter crown shall be her fate
> And yet her joy shall be more great.
> She shall be branded with men's blame,
> And for the glory wear the shame,
> Yet keep her spotless passion white
> Forever in all true men's sight.[6]

So the tragedy is predictable and inevitable: because it arises naturally from the personalities involved, it is impossible to avoid.

II *Guenevere: A Bitter Crown*

Guenevere's star had forecast a life both shameful and glorious, and her fate becomes the subject matter of the next play, *The Marriage of Guenevere*. This blank-verse tragedy shows considerable influence of Shakespeare; indeed, some of the lines seem to have been taken directly from *Hamlet*, *Othello*, or *Lear*. Hovey introduces the main characters—Arthur, Launcelot, and the usual entourage of the Table Round, as Tennyson was wont to call it—but Guenevere is the protagonist; and the action arises from her character.

It has already been mentioned that Guenevere is the person-ification of the "new woman," and one of the best speeches in the play is her soliloquy about women's rights:

> Why, what a thing is woman! She is brought
> Into the world unwelcome. The mother weeps
> That she has born a daughter to endure
> A woman's fate. The father knits his brows
> and mutters "Pish, 'tis but a girl."
>
> . . .
>
> She must be quiet,
> Demure—not have her freedom with the boys.
> While they are running on the battlements,
> Playing at war or at the chase, she sits
> Eating her heart out at embroidery frames
> Among old dames that chatter of a world
> Where women are put up as merchandise.
> —Oh, I have slipped away a thousand times
> Into the garden close and scaled the wall
> And fled from them to freedom and the hills.
> And I have passed the women in the fields,
> With stupid faces dulled by long restraint,
> Bowing their backs beneath the double burden
> Of labor and unkindness—all alike,
> Princes and peasant, bondslaves by their sex![7]

Guenevere, at the opening of the play, is skeptical about love. She has agreed to the marriage with Arthur because it is the will of her father, King Leodegrance. Merlin tells her that she will be the keystone of a great kingdom, and her mother secretly advises that it is unnecessary to remain faithful as long as she is discreet. So, thinks Guenevere, she might as well marry Arthur as another; but her brother, Peredure, counsels her otherwise. He knows what it means to have a hopeless love, and he warns her to keep her heart free to follow love whenever it might come.

Guenevere goes through with the marriage; but, before it can be consummated, Arthur is called away to suppress a rebellion. Launcelot returns from a journey and recognizes Guenevere as his mysterious love, the Lady of the Hills, who had nursed him one time when he was wounded. Launcelot says:

> Duty? The word is colder than the moon.
> Thou art an icy counsellor. Dost think
> That love will, like a hound that licks my hand,
> Down at my bidding? Nay, thou hast not loved,
> Nor dost not know that when Love enters in,
> He enters as a master, not a slave.[8]

Launcelot is caught in a dilemma between duty and love; but whatever he does will do harm, either to himself or to others. Love becomes stronger because Launcelot rationalizes that he is Guenevere's rightful lover because he saw her first and because he has won all the trophies for her. He tells her of this right when declaring his love, and she accepts him as her first lover and her real husband.

Jealous of her position, Guenevere's enemies begin to plot her downfall; they and the Romans bring a charge of treason against her which they hope will sunder the Round Table. Merlin realizes that he is responsible for the situation because he had originally suggested the marriage. The Queen whom he thought would provide stability for the state now proves to be the agent for its disintegration. After he wonders how this evil could have arisen from his good intentions, he decides that it was "Blind chance, that seems at times/ To have malevolent Intelligence."[9] But Arthur shows his magnanimity by dismissing the charges, for, since Launcelot is his closest friend, and Guenevere his Queen, he will believe no ill report about either.

Mrs. Hovey wrote that there are three Gueneveres: Tennyson's, who sins and later repents; William Morris' who appeals to human forgiveness; and Hovey's, "who only loves, who never sins, who never repents."[10] Although, in the eyes of society Guenevere violates a commandment, she does no wrong. Indeed, society was in the wrong because it had forced her into an arrangement against her will. Guenevere was only being true to herself; she was sanctified by her love.

III *Launcelot: Two Loyalties at War*

One of the liberties that Hovey takes with the legend is to make Galahad the child of Launcelot and Guenevere, for such parentage underscores one of the work's principal themes: that the greatest good is produced by the emotion of love. The stories of the birth of the son and of the war with Rome are intertwined in the next play, *The Birth of Galahad*, in which the action centers around Launcelot

as it had around Guenevere in the previous play. There is a definite
advance in blank verse technique, for Hovey has developed his own
style and no longer follows that of Shakespeare.

In Hovey's presentation, Launcelot is a much more tragic figure
than Guenevere, for she feels no allegiance to Arthur and rejoices in
her love with few pangs of guilt. Launcelot's conscience bothers him
much more; he and Arthur were as close as two men could be. Yet
Launcelot cannot give up Guenevere, for doing so would be an even
greater disloyalty. Because he is caught in a powerful tension between his two loves, his military conferences with the King are a
"daily torture":

> When Arthur puts his arm about my neck
> And tells me his imperial dreams, how he
> Will shape the world, when he has mastered it,
> To something worthier man's immortal soul,
> Keeping back nothing of his heart from me—
> Oh, Galahault, think how I love the man
> And how my heart must choke with its deceit!
> It were less miserable to confess to him—
> But that were tenfold more disloyalty
> To Guenevere than loyalty to him.
> Disloyalty! Oh, God, were I to break
> My promise to a slave, I'd hold myself
> A paltry and dishonored thing; and yet
> Whichever way I turn, disloyalty
> Yawns like a chasm before me.[11]

In Lyonnesse, Galahad is born on Easter Sunday. The Princess
Ylen pretends that he is her child, but Merlin arrives and sees
through the deceit. Guenevere defiantly admits her love; she is
proud of it; and the baby means more to her than the crown. Yet she
must lie to preserve the status quo, and her free spirit finds this
shame especially galling. When Merlin sees the baby Galahad, he
has a vision:

> I behold this child
> Grown to a man; the armor that he bears
> Is silvern pale; he stands among the knights
> Like a white birch among grim-visaged pines;
> He is like a moon-lit pillar in the night;
> And angels float unseen above his head,
> Bearing the Holy Graal.[12]

Merlin predicts that Galahad will be the peerless, stainless knight about whom the seers have spoken. He will prove dauntless, with an arm like David and with a sword like Michael. Guenevere then asks whether she has not sacrificed enough by allowing Ylen to raise Galahad.

The action of *Galahad*, developed through scenes of intrigue and plotting, is mainly concerned with the war against Rome. The Romans capture Guenevere and offer her to Launcelot as a prize. If he deserts Arthur, they will make him the king of Britain, and Guenevere can be his queen. But Launcelot, who always overcomes temptation, elects to serve Arthur while secretly loving Guenevere. In the end, the Britons triumph, and Arthur is crowned emperor by the Pope. Launcelot and Guenevere decide to terminate their affair and to sacrifice their love because of their obligations to the world.

IV *Taliesin: The Sacredness of Art*

Their renunciation was to be the subject of the second part of the cycle, but it was never written. Only the introduction, *Taliesin*, was completed. This masque, which suggests the esthetic drift of the cycle and which was not completed until 1896, contains some of Hovey's best poetry. Many excellent lyrics were included in anthologies. As in *Merlin*, Hovey employs a great variety of rhythms and meters, and he adapts the style to the speaker or singers. Taliesin himself, when his words are not set to song, speaks in a disciplined blank verse that allows him several imaginative flights.

The masque is concerned with the quest undertaken by Taliesin and young Sir Percival. They are seeking Merlin who, they believe, can tell them where to find the Graal. Percival tells Taliesin what Camelot has become:

> It has become a house of infamy.
> Ere I was made a knight, the sin I saw
> Make the light harsh and the air stifling to me;
> And then I vowed that my first knightly quest
> Should be to find some rescue from the sin.[13]

Percival reveals himself as a young man so pure that he cannot abide the thought of evil. He is unwilling to forgive his fellow men, and his hatred of their misdeeds makes him almost a misanthrope. Taliesin, on the other hand, is more compassionate and forgiving; he is willing to indulge the frailties of man. For this reason, he is allowed to progress farther toward the Graal than Percival.

Another reason, too, for Taliesin's progress is that he, as a poet, is interested in beauty. But he begins to realize during the quest that beauty is more than a pleasing sensation; it is also a creative, life-giving stimulant:

> As the heather glows over the hills
> Like a shadow ablaze,
> The moss of the forest-floor thrills
> Into blooms at thy gaze;
> The grasses begin to confer,
> And the crickets to fife;
> The borders of Death are astir
> With the armies of Life.[14]

Taliesin learns that, although the forms of literature and truth are many, the source is God. All art is revelation. God, a perfect spirit, is eternally revealing Himself. He speaks with the voices of nature; the harmony of the spheres attests to His powers of organization. He has also appeared through the pageant of history: empires, wars, and migrations reveal His purpose. Moreover, God reveals Himself through man, the clay out of which He molds the image of His dream. Taliesin then realizes that the world perceives these revelations through the agency of the poet:

> The myriad-wrought
> Harmonies of design and color fade
> For very intricacy of eloquence
> Into an indistinguishable gray.
> But bit by bit, if disentangled, held
> Apart, and shown to men, their eyes, once seeing
> The broken beauty isolated, turn
> Back to God's work to find it there forever;
> So God makes use of poets. Teach me, then,
> To fashion worlds in little, making form,
> As God does, one with spirit,—be the priest
> Who makes God into bread to feed the world.[15]

To transform the spirit of God into man becomes, therefore, the poet's mission.

Taliesin and Percival learn the legend of the Graal from its keeper, King Evelac; for it was brought to England by Joseph of Arimathea and entrusted to Evelac until the proper knight should come to receive it. When Percival announces that he is the one,

Evelac asks if he is the son of Ban. Percival replies that the son of Ban is Launcelot, who has no son and will never have one because he always remains faithful to some mysterious love. Because Percival has come by default, Evelac tells him not to take the oracles of God so lightly; for God will accomplish what He has promised. Percival is also told that he cannot see the Graal because his heart is too full of anger and because the hatred of evil clots his soul. Only when he has been made perfect by love can he appreciate the majestic Presence symbolized by the Graal; therefore, Percival is told to go back among his fellow men and to learn to love and forgive.

Compassion is a greater virtue than righteousness, and for this reason the revelation will be made to Taliesin. He is less perfect than Percival, but he has a sensitivity that the knight lacks. Because he is a poet and has the duty to communicate the divine Being to man, he will be given a glimpse of the ethereal beauty. Taliesin is admitted to the Presence, and he responds with a Hymn to Joy that praises eternal beauty, harmony, and aspiration:

> Under the teeth that clench and the eyes that weep,
> Deeper than discord or doubt or desire or wrong,
> One with the wills that sow and the Fates that reap,
> Joy in the heart of the world like a peal of song.
>
>   .   .   .
>
> Stir in the dark of the stars unborn that desire
> Only the thrill of a wild, dumb force set free,
> Yearn of the burning heart of the world on fire
> For life and birth and battle and wind and sea,
> Groping of life after love till the spirit aspire
> Into Divinity ever transmuting the clod,
> Higher and higher and higher and higher and higher
> Out of the Nothingness world without end into God.[16]

Taliesin is granted the privilege instead of Percival because his virtue comes from excess and not denial. Taliesin's power comes through consecration, Percival's through renunciation. The poet, wrote Mrs. Hovey, is the perfect man; for he combines the instinct of the body, the intelligence of the mind, and the aspiration of the soul "in capacity for joy in goodness."[17] He is a new type of hero. Medieval Christianity had culminated in the ascetic purity of knights such as Galahad, who had preserved civilization from barbarism; and the artist's goal is to liberate the puritanical nineteenth century from this asceticism.

When *Taliesin* appeared, Curtis Hidden Page, in a perceptive review, called the masque a "poet's poem" that was really about the training and discipline of the artist. In his quest, Taliesin was conducted to various levels of meaning by figures from Celtic and Classical mythology. What Hovey is saying is that modern poetry is a combination of the passionate lyricism of the Celtic poetry and the rational discipline of the Classic.[18] Depth of feeling is not·enough; in order for poetry to communicate, it must be worked into form and structure.

V *Fragments*

Although *Taliesin* is the last completed piece of the cycle, enough fragments of the unfinished plays exist to give an idea of the total work. The several scenes and speeches of *The Holy Graal* that are extant indicate that this play tells of the vision of the Graal received by the guilt-ridden court and of the several knights who take vows of chastity and who begin their individual quests to restore the golden age to Camelot. In one completed scene, Launcelot discusses the vows with Dubric, Archbishop of Canterbury. When the clergyman commends Launcelot for taking up the cause because all the knights respect him, Launcelot admits that he is doing so because of his need to cleanse himself from sin. He once had a quarrel with the world; and, because he had believed the world had done him wrong, he had put it aside and followed his own desire. But he now recognizes how this individual and selfish course can harm his comrades. Dubric admits that it is very difficult to know when men's wills are pure because self-interest often masquerades as conscience, but he states that the only agency that can distinguish proper motives from improper ones is the church. As a result, Launcelot accepts the guidance of the church and dedicates himself to the cause.

As is obvious from Hovey's notes, *The Holy Graal* was to be about masculine purity. Galahad is contrasted with the other knights who become seduced from their vows; but, though he is able to resist temptation, he is not a prude. If he remains a virgin, he does so because he meets no woman whose spirituality of passion matches his. Purity, according to Hovey, does not deny the passionate, only the sensual. "It will be readily understood by all who knew Richard

Hovey that he could not have intended to show that Galahad, the typical knight of purity, should have attained his height through any ascetic or otherwise morbid ideal of life. Not by living less than the best but by living all things better than the best is the whiteness of the soul attained."[19] Galahad's whiteness—the whiteness of light— is comprised of all colors. He lives in the world but is not of it. In *Taliesin*, it had been predicted of him that he could walk in the mire but not be stained.

The intentions of the remaining unfinished plays can be quickly summarized. In *Astolat*, Guenevere and Launcelot were to be re- united after their renunciations had failed. *Fata Morgana*, the "masque of evil" that was to introduce Part III, was to show Launcelot's becoming a monk. *Morte d'Arthur* would see the fall of the Round Table and the death of Arthur, but all problems were to be resolved in *Avalon*, the legendary island tomb of Arthur and the heaven of the romances. Here all desires would be fulfilled: Launcelot and Guenevere would be recognized as rightful lovers; Arthur would be married to a more suitable queen; even Galahad would discover his ideal mate.

The masque *Merlin* had raised the problem of individual destiny, for each soul had been compared to a separate star. Now in the last play the metaphysical assumptions underlying the whole work become explicit: the ether in which the stars move is God Himself. His power is love, which is the force that holds each star, or indi- vidual spirit, in its place and brings about a harmony of destinies. Whenever love is thwarted in some way, disharmony arises. Since there are several gradations of love, it proves more harmful to vio- late a greater love than a lesser one. Launcelot explains all this metaphysics to Guenevere:

> I love my fellows as earth loves the stars
> That move far off in their own silent courses,
> Shedding on us a mild beneficence;
> Others I love as earth loves Uranus,
> Mars, Venus, Mercury, Saturn, and the sun.
> For these are nearer to me and their courses
> Inextricably intertwined with mine.
> But thee, my sweet, my greatest heart of women,
> Thee do I love as the earth loves the moon.[20]

Launcelot's tragedy is that his star is pulled by two other stars in opposite directions: he is torn between friendship and allegiance on one hand and passionate love on the other. Guenevere is as helpless as he; she either has to degrade Arthur and Launcelot or herself. The solution lies outside her power, for the lines of fate are already drawn. Even Christianity with its doctrine of renunciation is of no use because personalities cannot renounce themselves any more than the sun can renounce its shining. Arthur is the only one who can renounce anything, and his ambition has made him so insensitive to others that he does not know what is happening. The tragedy lies in the fact that the earthly social arrangement does not match the harmony of the heavenly spheres.

Mrs. Hovey explained that the *Poem in Dramas* was not undertaken to excuse Launcelot and Guenevere, nor to demonstrate Arthur's psychic blindness, but to "impeach the social system that had not yet—and has not yet—gone far enough in evolution to become a medium in which all lives can move at all times and in all respects in freedom. This surely is the ideal."[21] The real culprit, then, is the puritanical society with its material values and conforming pressures and with its denial of the passionate (spiritual) element of life.

Hovey's contemporaries were not fooled into thinking that he had written another Medieval romance.[22] His characters were different from Tennyson's—they were modern. Guenevere was certainly the "new woman," and Arthur and Launcelot were also modern. They were alive with modern problems—especially the conflict between individual and social interests. Hovey was apparently successful in getting his theme across, and he also appears to be one of the first American writers to use a myth to present modern themes. Poets of the past, of course, have used myth and legend for subject matter; they have usually incorporated into the works the problems of their eras; but they were probably not as deliberate as modern writers. This conscious use of myth to clarify contemporary experience is one of the hallmarks of modern literature, for the myth can help the writers give real experience a deeper perspective. The reader of today has seen myth used in many ways in James Joyce's *Ulysses*, in T. S. Eliot's *Waste Land*, in Thomas Mann's *Joseph and His Brothers*, in William Faulkner's *The Hamlet*, and in John Updike's *The Centaur*. But Hovey wrote before Yeats, Joyce, and Eliot made the approach popular; and his conscious decision to use the Arthurian myth to present a modern theme prepared the way for writers of today.

VI *Ontology of Love*

Since the *Poem in Dramas* is Hovey's longest and most systematic work, it contains the best presentation of his philosophy. In this work, his ontological statements indicate where Hovey thought reality was located. Among his songs praising Nature, Taliesin addresses one to the stars; and he notes how they dwell apart and move separately. But they are united by the "formless ether" and can communicate with each other through ether waves. This ether-wave concept would scarcely be acceptable today after Max Planck and Albert Einstein, but to Hovey the use of such a theory was for symbolic reasons since the stars are really individual souls:

> The centered Soul
> By these is known.
> Its will it wreaks
> At its own control;
> But dumb, unseeing,
> The sea of Being
> Washes the peaks
> Where it strives above.[23]

Taliesin then addresses this Sea of Being. Everything individual has been created from it—"struck from the solution," as Walt Whitman said; and the tides of Being still hold tight to the individual pieces. In this Sea of Being, the "lonely mind" discovers its depth and also its relation with universal existence. Here in this ultimate source of Being lies fundamental and essential truth; all other is incidental and partial.

To Hovey, the idealist, the so-called material world is but a dumb manifestation of the real world underneath. This spiritual reality is the life principle of the universe:

> Through the manifold forms of His moulding
> It streams, and its working is rife,
> Forever enfleshed and unfolding—
> Life, life![24]

But Hovey, who was a Christian idealist, goes one step farther when he identifies this spiritual reality with God; and, in so doing, he ascribes beneficent and creative characteristics to it. The Muses tell Taliesin that God is a perfect spirit Who is eternally revealing

Himself, and history is the revelation of His word. The universe is His garment, and the soul of man His image. His power is the natural law of the universe—the force that holds all individual stars in orbit—and this power is also known as "love." Launcelot tells Guenevere:

> The atmosphere of souls, the ether
> In which they swim like stars, is God himself.
> In Him they live and move and have their being.
> The power that holds each spirit in its place
> And melts the heaven of souls in harmony
> Is love that draws each spirit to its neighbor;
> And as the various spaces of the stars,
> So soul from soul is variously severed.[25]

Love, then, is the organizing force of the universe; and the social fabric is dependent upon it. When individuals act out of self-interest, they disrupt the harmony necessary for life. To achieve this essential harmony individuals must remain in their own place, have respect for their fellow souls, and have reverence for the cords that unite them with the Sea of Being.

Arthur, on one occasion, argues about the necessity for the unified state that Britain had become under him. If each barony, each shire, would have sovereignty, there would be nothing but disorder:

> Why, such a land is like a rotting corpse;
> For when that harmony and principle
> Of union, which is life, is ta'an away,
> And each corporeal atom works alone,
> The issue is corruption.[26]

The social order is similar, therefore, to the physical world; it too needs love to keep things in place.

The importance that Hovey assigns to love can be seen throughout the plays. It is much more than a passion; it is a redeeming and creative force. Morgause pleads with her lover to forsake his vows of chastity because love had saved her: "love reconciles all ill."[27] Peredure, in wondering about his love, doubts that it could be sinful because it has made him "greater-hearted than before."[28] Guenevere does not believe she has sinned; she is only ashamed that she has to keep her love hidden. She tells Merlin that she is prouder of her love than of her crown. Love is also responsible for Launcelot's great works; his heroism arises from his great passion. Launcelot tells Guenevere that their love did not originate within their wills but "from the will of God—for every effect / Must have a will somewhere behind it."[29] Since their love was heaven-sent, it could not be bad. Love, then, is something good because it has a beneficent effect.

VII   *Salvation through Sin*

Despite its great beneficent force, love can certainly cause problems. *Launcelot and Guenevere* was conceived as a study in ethics: to determine what was real virtue and what was sin. All the ethical problems are generated by love. Launcelot is in the central position; he does not know whether to be true to his desires, to Guenevere's love for him, or to his friendship for Arthur. The decision is all the more complex because of the value Hovey places upon both individuality and comradeship. It is just as sinful to violate one's own integrity as it is to violate the bonds of friendship. Launcelot realizes that whatever he does will do harm, either to himself or to others. Due to the complexity of the situation, he can find no clear solution to his problem:

> True is false,
> And false is true; and everything that is,
> A mocking contradiction of itself.[30]

No matter what he does, he sins.

Sin, however, operates according to the dialectic process. When a man has over-indulged in one type of sin, the pendulum swings in the other direction. Launcelot admits to the priest Dubric that he has taken up the quest for the Graal because sin has rent his heart:

> I had a quarrel with the world;
> It had done me wrong; therefore I put it by
> And took my own, or so I thought. But now,
> Even to take my own, I would not do
> This evil to my fellows.[31]

Launcelot has reached the point where he will sacrifice his desires for the good of society.

Although Hovey's position is that it is impossible to live without sin, he is not a Calvinist. He does not believe in natural depravity. On one occasion the clown Dagonet picks up the baby Galahad and says: "who would think that this was a monster of iniquity, not yet washed from his sins, and I one of the saints, clean as a fresh laundered shirt, absolved o' Saturday, communicated o' Sunday, and not having had a chance to commit any sins since?"[32] When the reader remembers that the fool Dagonet is hardly perfect and that the baby he is talking about is Galahad, who will grow to be a matchless example of purity, he finds it easy to perceive the irony in the speech. Man is not born evil, but evil comes about as a natural consequence of life.

The only way a man could escape sin would be to withdraw from life and activity entirely—as the Voices of Sleep advise Taliesin to do:

> Sleep, and renounce the vital day;
> For evil is the child of life.
> Let be the will to live, and pray
> To find forgetfulness of strife.[33]

They advise him to withdraw into the thicket where there is no light to discriminate good from evil; and where no sin exists because there is no individuality. When the individual self becomes united with Being, or Nature as it is called here, "There shall be no more sin to hate."

Taliesin does not listen to the voices but goes on to see infinite goodness filtered through the Graal. In fact, he is allowed to see this purity because he has sinned, because he is human. In writing about the plays of Maeterlinck, Hovey remarked that the dramatist's greatest triumph was his characterization of goodness. "For the goodness of Maeterlinck's people is real goodness and not priggishness."[34] There can be monsters of goodness just as there can be monsters of evil. Percival's goodness is the wrong kind; it does not come from overcoming temptations in life but from renouncing life altogether. True virtue is that which has experienced life and evil.

CHAPTER 5

Along the Trail

NOT until 1898 did Hovey publish his first solo book of verse—
Along the Trail. Because it covers so many different phases of
his career, the volume is his most representative. There are early
efforts, written in college and even before. Some of the pieces had
appeared, in slightly different form, in the *Vagabondias*. The book
also includes the Dartmouth and fraternity songs that Hovey had
written for alumni occasions, as well as the Spanish-American War
poems.

I *Patriotism*

Hovey apparently felt no contradiction between his Bohemian
life-style and his love of country. In fact, he might have argued that
the dissenter from the middle-class values of commercialism and
materialism was the real patriot. The outcasts, such as Walt
Whitman, were the ones who were keeping the ideals of true
Americanism alive. Most Americans had forgotten the meaning of
their own Revolution, and the nation had neglected its duty to the
oppressed of the world. The destruction of the battleship "Maine"
was both a punishment and a message sent by God to remind
America of its destiny—as Hovey makes clear in "The Word of the
Lord from Havana":

> Thus spake the Lord:
> Because ye have not heard,
> Because ye have given no heed
> To my people in their need,
>
> Because the oppressed cried
> From the dust where he died,
> And ye turned your face away
> From his cry in that day,

Because ye have bought and sold
That which is above gold,
Because your brother is slain
While ye get you drunk with gain,

      .   .   .

Therefore my
Angel of Death
Hath stretched out his hand on you,
Therefore I speak in my wrath,
Laying command on you;

      .   .   .

Ye who held peace less than right
When a king laid a pitiful tax on you,
Hold not your hand from the fight
When Freedom cries under the axe on you!

(I who called France to you, call you to
   Cuba in turn!
Repay—lest I cast you adrift and you perish
   astern!)

      .   .   .

Ye who remembered the Alamo,
Remember the Maine!
Ye who unfettered the slave,
Break a free people's chain![1]

"The Call of the Bugles," which contains most of Hovey's thoughts about the war, begins with short lines and a militant beat that represents the angry spirit of the country. From North and South alike a mighty army has come, for the "old sap of fight" still runs in America's veins. When the tempo shifts to the reverie of taps, it echoes back in time much farther than the recent November afternoon when Hovey buried his soldier-father at Arlington; he hears the "ghostly roll of immaterial drums" as the tread of "the great armies of the Past go by." Across the years the sound carries from Concord and Valley Forge, and the cheer rises from Vicksburg. America can best honor these dead by continuing with heroic deeds like theirs.

Cuba's worst enemy has not been Spain but the international financiers, who include the monopolists of Wall Street. But the greedy exploitation of these capitalists has been exposed, and America can now hear the Word of the Lord. Now that the truth is known, America can play the role of God's avenging angel, punish Spain, and set the people of Cuba free. There is no hope for Spain; for the European nations, such as Germany, who have declaimed against American intervention will not be able to prevent America's righteous purpose. Besides, there is the Monroe Doctrine, which Hovey describes:

> For the writ of the Powers does not run
> Where the flag of the Union floats.
> Fair and equal every one
> We greet with loyal throats;
> But we own no suzerain.
> Thewed with freedom,
> Mailed in destiny—
> We shall maintain
> Against the world our right,
> Their peer in majesty, their peer in might.[2]

In fact, America is greater than the nations of Europe because they are "Rothschild-ridden" and have sold their flags for gold. England alone is honorable; she supports the American cause (and her own interest). France has forgotten Lafayette and her ancient allegiance; her shame will come in time.

America's implied purpose in the war goes even beyond the liberation of Cuba, for her intervention between Cuba and Spain signals to the world that she is ready to protect the weak from the strong. Those domestic critics who think the state is wrong in punishing an evildoer should stop their unmanly talk of peace and unite in the common cause against wrong. Peace can come when there is no more tyranny, but until then—war. War is necessary and even holy:

> Great is war—great and fair!
> The terrors of his face are grand and sweet,
> And to the wise the calm of God is there.
> God clothes himself in darkness as in light,
> —The God of love, but still the God of might.

Those who do the work of fighting do not love less; it is through their work that advancement comes; and the bugle call is the beating of the nation's heart:

> By strife as well as loving—strife,
> The Law of Life,—
> In brute and man the climbing has been done
> And shall be done hereafter. Since man was,
> No upward-climbing cause
> Without the sword has ever yet been won.

Hovey's belief that progress is accomplished only by strife and battle is expressed in a more condensed fashion in the sonnet "America." America was conceived in violence, and the nation should not shirk from war in order to accomplish its mission:

> We came to birth in battle; when we pass,
> It shall be to the thunder of the drums.
> We are not one that weeps and saith Alas,
> Nor one that dreams of dim millenniums.
> Our hand is set to this world's business,
> And it must be accomplished workmanly;
> Be we not stout enough to keep our place,
> What profits it the world that we be free?
> Not with despite for others, but to hold
> Our station in the world inviolate,
> We keep the stomach of the men of old
> Who built in blood the bastions of our fate.
> We know not to what goal God's purpose tends;
> We know He works through battle to His ends.[3]

II *Love Poems*

Although Hovey is remembered today (if at all) as a poet of un-inhibited meters and rhymes, many of his best poems are sonnets. He experimented with all varieties of the form throughout his career, and in his mature years he seemed especially challenged by the discipline required to advance, develop, and conclude a theme within one hundred and forty syllables of sound; to obey strict metrical and rhythmic rules; and to follow an intricate rhyme pattern. Hovey adapted the form to many different subjects— nature, politics, religion, and philosophy—but his most frequent theme was love. He did not forget that the purpose of the sonnet (as defined by Sir Philip Sidney) was to win a mistress.

The sonneteers of the Middle Ages exalted their loved ones. The tradition of Courtly Love was to raise the lady on a pedestal and to have the lover grovel at her feet while swearing undying fealty. Medieval love was idealized and apparently immortal, but Hovey examines the permanence of love from a modern view in a cycle of three Petrarchan sonnets titled "Love and Change." The first lover rationalizes that all love is ephemeral: since it is conceived in passion, it will naturally decline; and neither prayer nor tears can restore it. The argument of the second lover is a paradox of idealism and selfishness. He once believed that love is eternal, but experience has taught him otherwise. But he has not changed; he has always remained in love, but the objects of his affection, his paramours, have changed. The third lover, who combines practicality with idealism, realizes that, while love will diminish, it can be renewed for the same person because that person will be growing and changing too:

> My love for you dies many times a year,
>   And a new love is monarch in his place.
>   Love must grow weary of the fairest face;
> The fondest heart must fail to hold him near.
> For love is born of wonder, kin to fear—
>   Things grown familiar lose the sweet amaze;
>   Grown to their measure, love must turn his gaze
> To some new splendor, some diviner sphere.
> But in the blue night of your endless soul
>   New stars globe ever as the old are scanned;
>   Goal where love will, you reach a farther goal,
> And the new love is ever love of you.
>   Love needs a thousand loves, forever new,
>   And finds them—in the hollow of your hand.[4]

This sonnet introduces a theme that Hovey repeatedly uses—love as an exploration. Love is the opposite of selfishness; for, because of love, a person not only cares for others and thinks less about self but gets to know them better. Love, the key which also unlocks other personalities, helps a person learn their interests, desires, and concerns. Love, then, is the moral agent necessary for overcoming the narrowness of self-concern and self-pity; and it elevates the lover above the pettiness of the everyday world as is indicated in "After Business Hours."

> When I sit down with thee at last alone,
>   Shut out the wrangle of the clashing day,
>   The scrape of petty jars that fret and fray,
>   The snarl and yelp of brute beasts for a bone;

When thou and I sit down at last alone,
   And through the dusk of rooms divinely gray
   Spirit to spirit finds its voiceless way,
   As tone melts meeting in accordant tone,—
Oh, then our souls, far in the vast of sky,
   Look from a tower, too high for sound of strife
   Or any violation of the town,
Where the great vacant winds of God go by,
   And over the huge misshapen city of life
   Love pours his silence and his moonlight down.[5]

Those who criticize love as mere passion or as something bestial do not understand its ennobling powers. There is a religious aspect about love that really makes the lover more divine. Thus, Hovey does agree with that part of the Courtly Love tradition that conceived love to be a refining agent, making men better than they were before. He also agrees that love makes men more courageous, ready to slay dragons and to rescue damsels fair.

This idea is developed in "Love in the Winds," another sonnet, one that uses the imagery of war. In it, Hovey employs one of his most frequent metaphors, comparing love to a ship carrying two people to some unknown destiny. Love, an all-or-nothing venture, is "to be" or "not to be." The poem opens with the image of a ship's bow that rises over and plunges through waves as it "sniffs the storm," but it concludes with the sinking amid waves that rise like "clashing spears":

The ship we ride the world in sniffs the storm.
And throws its head up to the hurricane,
Quivering like a war-horse when ranks form
With scream of bugles and the shout of men,
Neighs to the challenge of the thunderbolt,
And charges in the squadrons of the surge,
Sabring its way with fury of revolt
And lashed with exaltation as a scourge!
Who would not rather founder in the fight
Than not have known the glory of the fray?
Ay, to go down in armor and in might,
With our last breath to dominate dismay,
So sink amid the mad sea's clashing spears
And with the cry of bugles in our ears![6]

The concept of love as expressed in Hovey's sonnets is more spiritual than physical because love is the agent which can elevate man's moral parts. It destroys selfishness, stimulates the imagination, and brings comfort; it can make a person more courageous and daring; it can overcome vicissitude; and it gives strength, happiness, and well-being. One might say that love is the condition of the heart that breeds virtue. In fact, Hovey's idea of love is similar to that expressed by St. Paul in the thirteenth chapter of Corinthians.

Although Hovey's love poetry does seem to reflect many values of Courtly Romance, he does add to it the modern theme of individuality. Just as *Launcelot and Guenevere* is really a modern drama in ancient dress, so do the love poems show the modern concern for individual rights. In two poems, "The Love of a Boy—Yesterday" and "The Love of a Boy—Today," Hovey contrasts the two types of love. The first poem celebrates the Medieval tradition of the knight's swearing eternal loyalty to his lady:

> No lips nor lutes can let thee know
> The joy that lightens through my woe,—
> But look in thine own heart, and so
> I shall not need to tell thee, love.
>> Lady of the winsome smile!
>> Lovesome lady! Gentle lady!
>> If my heart had any guile,
>> Thou wouldst make me truthful, love.
>
> Though bitter be our luckless lot,
> It were more sad if love were not—
> And all the rest may be forgot,
> But thou wilt not forget me, love—
>> Lady of the faithful heart!
>> Loving lady! Loyal lady!
>> Were I noble as thou art,
>> No king's sword need knight me, love.
>
> Were I myself a mighty king
> With thousands at my beckoning,
> My power were but a little thing
> To do thee worthy honor, love.
>> Lady in whose life I live!
>> Fearless lady! Peerless lady!
>> If the stars were mine to give
>> They should be thy necklace, love.[7]

Such a love is self-denying; the lover prostrates himself completely and love becomes a responsibility. But modern love, which is so different, leads the lover away from responsibility and duty. Modern love brings him freedom and stimulates his imagination. Love is denial of the ordinary world, for love is all-consuming, as the second poem implies:

> Heigh-Ho! my thoughts are far away;
> For wine or books I have no care;
> I like to think upon the way
> She has of looking very fair.
>> Oh, work is nought, and play is nought,
>> And all the livelong day is nought;
>> There's nothing much I care to learn
>> But what her lovely lips have taught.
>
> The campus cannot tempt me out,
> The classics cannot keep me in;
> The only place I care about
> Is where perchance she may have been.
>> Oh, work is nought, and play is nought,
>> And all the livelong day is nought;
>> There's nothing much I care to find
>> Except the way she would be sought.
>
> The train across the valley screams,
> And like a hawk sweeps out of sight;
> It bears me to her in my dreams
> By day and night, by day and night.
>> Oh, work is nought, and play is nought,
>> And all the livelong day is nought;
>> There's nothing much I care to be,
>> If I be only in her thought.[8]

Along the Trail contains several translations of sonnets by Mallarmé that Hovey had done in France. The traditional sonnet themes of love, mutability, and death were easily suited to the dominant mood of melancholy found in Symbolist poetry. Hovey's translations are important, not because they introduced the French movement to a wider audience, but because they show a stylistic development toward greater utilization of imagery. In the sonnet "Summer Sadness," the shimmering golden summer makes distinctions unreal; and sun, water, and hair become almost the same. In such an atmosphere, the lovers find it possible to weep incense, drink air, and drown in hair in an attempt to find some balm for the pain of death and separation:

> The sunlight on the sands, fair struggler fallen asleep,
>   Makes warm a bath of languors in your golden hair,
> And, burning away the angry incense that you weep,
>   Mingles a wanton drink of longings in the air.
>
> Immutable in calm, the white flamboyant day
>   Has made you sigh (alas, my kisses full of qualms!)
> "No, we shall never be one mummy, swathed for aye
>   Under the ancient desert and the happy palms."
>
> This incubus of soul we suffer, in the river
> Of your warm hair might plunge and drown without a shiver,
> And find that Nothingness that you know nothing of,
>   And I would taste those tears of rouge beneath your eyes,
> To see if they can give the heart you smote with love
>   The insensibility of stones and summer skies.[9]

All in all, Hovey made an important contribution to American poetry by using love as the subject of his poems. In examining anthologies of American verse, the student finds only a few poems about love before 1890. Of course, there are Poe's necrophilia (such as "Ulalume") and such narratives as Whittier's "Maud Muller" and Longfellow's "Evangeline," but these are hardly intimate, passionate lyrics. Both Whitman and Emily Dickinson used love but for symbolic purposes: Whitman, for democratic aims; Dickinson, for life experience. The changed love poetry after Hovey's career is represented by the poems of Elinor Wylie, Hilda Doolittle, Edna St. Vincent Millay, Robinson Jeffers, e e cummings, and Ezra Pound. Love even creeps into the austere New England line—E. A. Robinson, Robert Frost, Amy Lowell, and T. S. Eliot. This poetry differs from the earlier variety, by being more sensual and realistic.

Hovey is, however, hardly responsible for this change that also exists in the American novel. During the 1890's new theories of love and sex were developing, theories based more on human behavior than on abstract morals. Customs also were changing because people began to accept divorce as a solution for an unhappy marriage. It was only a matter of time before these modern opinions would be reflected in art. Hovey wanted to use love for subject matter, and he was bold enough to break through the barrier set up

by the Genteel Tradition. He took a step forward, and his example
no doubt gave others courage.

III *Dartmouth Lyrics*

Allan Macdonald gives Hovey credit for articulating the myth of
Dartmouth: "It is as if he created the present Dartmouth, the
Dartmouth of myth . . . a pagan, Anglo-Saxon myth of primitive
living and comradeship quite unlike that of Latin piety toward Alma
Mater."[10] The spirit of the famous Winter Carnival is expressed in
the "Hanover Winter Song," which was set to music by Hovey's
friend, Frederick Field Bullard, and which has remained a favorite
with men's choral groups. It is developed by two contrasting series
of images—outside and indoors. Those of the outside relate the
fierce northern winter, the ice and snow, the "wolf-wind" that wails
at the door, and the "great white cold!" which walks abroad. The
indoor imagery creates the mood of warmth and friendship:

> Ho, a song by the fire!
> (Pass the pipes, fill the bowl!)
> Ho, a song by the fire!
> —With a skoal!
>
> . . .
>
> For the wolf-wind is whining in the doorways,
> And the snow drifts deep along the road,
> And the ice-gnomes are marching from their Norways,
> And the great white cold walks abroad.
> (Boo-oo-o! pass the bowl!)
>   For here by the fire
>   We defy frost and storm.
>   Ha, ha! we are warm
> And we have our hearts' desire;
>   For here's four good fellows
>   And the beechwood and the bellows,
>   And the cup is at the lip
>   In the pledge of fellowship.
>   Skoal![11]

Most of the Dartmouth songs were written to be read at various
alumni or fraternity reunions, and "Men of Dartmouth" won the
prize in a contest to find a suitable song for the college. As Macdonald indicates, Hovey disregarded the traditional alma mater
approach and wrote a new type of college song—one built upon the

physical elements of the college. In "Men of Dartmouth," Hovey refers to the harsh New England weather, the rugged granite hills, and even to the Lone Pine which was a college landmark. To the poet, the invigorating environment had made the men of Dartmouth tough and rugged, able to strive against hardship and to overcome obstacles. They were like the Vikings of old; and, in the final stanza, Hovey calls for a continuation of the tradition:

> Men of Dartmouth, give a rouse
> For the college on the hill!
> For the Lone Pine above her
> And the loyal men who love her—
>   For the sons of Dartmouth,
>   The sturdy sons of Dartmouth—
>   Though round the girdled earth they roam,
>   Her spell on them remains;
>   They have the still North in their hearts,
>   The hill-winds in their veins,
>   And the granite of New Hampshire
>   In their muscles and their brains.
>
> They were mighty men of old
> That she nurtured at her side,
> Till like Vikings they went forth
> From the lone and silent North—
> And they strove, and they wrought, and they died
>   But—the sons of old Dartmouth,
>   The laureled sons of Dartmouth—
>   The Mother keeps them in her heart
>   And guards their altar-flame;
>   The still North remembers them,
>   The hill-winds know their name,
>   And the granite of New Hampshire
>   Keeps the record of their fame.
>
> Men of Dartmouth, set a watch
> Lest the old traditions fail!
> Stand as brother stands by brother!
> Dare a deed for the old Mother!
> Greet the world, from the hills, with a hail!
>   For the sons of old Dartmouth,
>   The loyal sons of Dartmouth—
>   Around the world they keep for her
>   Their old chivalric faith;

> They have the still North in their souls,
> The hill-winds in their breath;
> And the granite of New Hampshire
> Is made part of them till death.[12]

Colleges have been traditionally known as foster mothers, and Hovey uses throughout his lyrics the son-mother relationship to explain the students' affection for the college. One poem that develops this idea of filial devotion to some extent is "A Winter Thought of Dartmouth in Manhattan." Written to be read at an alumni banquet, the poem compares the little college in New Hampshire with the great mercantile metropolis. The alumni think of their "Mother off in the hills, by the banks of the beautiful river." But they do not return to her because they have left "as men leave mothers."

Men leave mothers to marry wives, and the alumni have found their love. "She that sits by the sea,"—Manhattan—has her great harbors, her tall buildings, and the flags of all nations flying from the masts of ships. Hovey then attempts a poetic description of Manhattan that is somewhat reminiscent of Walt Whitman before him and that also foreshadows Hart Crane in *The Bridge*:

> Look how the line of her roofs coming down from the north
> Breaks into surf-leap of granite—jagged sierras—
> Upheaval volcanic, lined sharp on the violet sky
> Where the red moon, lop-sided, past the full,
> Over their ridge swims in the tide of space,
> And the harbor waves laugh softly, silently.
>> Look, how the overhead train at the Morningside curve
>> Looks like a sea-dragon its sinuous flight,
>> Loops in the night in and out, high up in the air,
>> Like a serpent of stars with the coil and undulant reach of the waves—
> From under the Bridge at noon
> See from the yonder shore how the great curves rise and converge,
> Like the beams of the universe, like the masonry of the sky,
> Like the arches set for the corners of the world,
> The foundation-stone of the orbic spheres and spaces.[13]

The city is both beautiful and tempting; few have the power to resist her, and a number of Dartmouth's sons have come to her. Yet they have not forgotten their mother or the time of their youth. Just as the sprout lives on in the bough, their letters that they send from

Manhattan reveal the love of a boy in the heart of a man. Their
letters are their offerings in remembrance of the hills and the river,
the old halls, and the rooms where others are now singing and
forming friendships.

A more imaginative use of the female image occurs in "Our Liege
Lady, Dartmouth" in which Hovey establishes a Courtly Love relationship. In this poem, the college becomes the Queen of Love;
and the students and alumni are the knights who would win her
honor. Just as the Medieval knights became more powerful through
their love, the students will because of theirs. Also, like the knights,
they will strive harder to win that fame which is really praise for
their queen; and, conversely, they will achieve it because of her
purity:

> Up with the green! Comrades, our Queen
> Over the hill-tops comes to convene
>   Liege men all to her muster.
> Easy her chain! Blithe be her reign,
> Queened in our heart's love, never a strain
>   Dimming her 'scutcheon's lustre!
> Up with the green! God save our Queen!
> Throned on the hills of her highland demesne,
> Royal and beautiful, wise and serene,
>   Our Liege Lady, Dartmouth![14]

Hovey's loyalty to Dartmouth was not a blind devotion. That he
could be critical of the institution is shown by the "Dartmouth
Ode," written for the college's one hundred and twenty-fifth an-
niversary.[15] This poem reflects his bias against the science and the
technology that might eventually destroy Nature. To Hovey, the
natural setting of Dartmouth had contributed to its great history; it
had graduated Daniel Webster among other famous men. But the
college should not be content with its laurels of the past; it should
plan for the future. Colleges do well enough to develop magnanimity and compassion in students and to educate for sensitivity.
Education of the heart is as important as that of the mind, and this
can be best achieved in close proximity with Nature. In the covering
letter that Hovey sent to Dartmouth's President Tucker with the
poem, he explained that he was not criticizing his Alma Mater
because he lacked pride in her. In fact, he had stated in the ode that
none loved her more. But he wanted to see his college as something

more than a competent institution; he wanted it to be an educational leader.[16]

It has already been mentioned that Hovey was a loyal member of Psi Upsilon all his life; and he recited poems written especially for conventions of the fraternity. The first time he performed was at the sixtieth convention held at Dartmouth in 1893, and the poem that he read was the long free-verse "Comrades." This poem opens with Hovey's joy at being able to return to Dartmouth:

> Again among the hills!
> The shaggy hills!
> The clear arousing air comes like a call
> Of bugle notes across the pines, and thrills
> My heart as if a hero had just spoken.
> Again among the hills!
> Far off, Ascutney smiles as one at peace;
> And over all
> The golden sunlight pours, and fills
> The hollow of the earth, like a god's joy.
> Again among the hills!
> The tranquil hills
> That took me as a boy
> And filled my spirit with the silences![17]

The hills are permanent fixtures, untouched by the anxious cares of man—his ambitions, strivings, and conflicts. The poet, however, has been shaped also by other forces such as the Lone Pine, the village streets, the athletic fields, the classrooms, and even those "spectacled comic unrelated beings," those science students who live apart in a strange land of "ohms and logarithms." But more important to his development than either the fortitude learned from the environment or the knowledge gained in the classroom was friendship:

> But more than strength and more than truth
> Oh, praise the love of man and man!
> Praise it for pledge of our eternal youth!
> Praise it for pulse of that great gush that ran
> Through all the worlds, when He
> Who made them clapped His hands for glee,
> And laughed Love down the cycle of the stars.
> Praise all that plants it in the hearts of men,

> All that protects it from the hoof that mars,
> The weed that stifles; praise the rain
> That rains upon it and the sun that shines,
> Till it stretch skyward with its laden vines!
> Praise then for thee, Psi Upsilon!

The fraternity is important because it begins and nourishes friendships. It concerns itself with other values too, the cultivation of the mind, art and letters; but its primary function is to encourage "the love of comrades." Friendship is a value often overlooked or taken for granted, but it should not be.

This theme of friendship is then reinforced by the lyric, "Comrades, Pour the Wine To-night," that Hovey later used for the conclusion of *Vagabondia* (See Chapter 1). Following the lyric is a fable about youth and decision where three women offer power, wisdom, or love. Hovey's advice is that love is more important than the other two. The poem then fades into the imagery of night that brings peace and contentment.

> Dark mother-night, draw near;
> Lay hands on us and whisper words of cheer
> So softly, oh, so softly! Now may we
> Be each as one that leaves his midnight task
> And throws his casement open; and the air
> Comes up across the lowlands from the sea
> And cools his temples, as a maid might ask
> With shy caress what speech would never dare;
> And he leans back to her demure desires,
> And as a dream sees far below
> The city with its lights aglow,
> And blesses in his heart his brother there;
> Then toward the eternal stars again aspires.

Once more Hovey affirms with this poem the necessity of comradeship: creative work which begins in brotherly love is best.

The poem was written to be read aloud; and there can be little doubt that Hovey's fine voice added greatly to the piece. So successful was the presentation that he was invited to perform again at the sixty-third fraternity convention at the University of Michigan in May, 1896; and the poem—"Spring"—written for this occasion paid his way home from Europe. He decided to use the same format that had been so successful three years before: the long poem in rhymed free verse with a lyric insert. "The muse was rebellious, not to say balky, at the start," he wrote a friend; "but by dint of persuading her that we were not bound for Ann Arbor at all but only for an old-time ramble in the woods at our own sweet will, I got her to begin."[18]

Bliss Carman has related how Hovey worked. He would shut himself in a room, perhaps for days at a time, with only a typewriter and a supply of tobacco. He would go over the poem again and again in his mind until he had its organization, making no notes of ideas of fragmentary lines. Once he had a few lines clear, he would sit at the typewriter to write them. Then he would rise from his chair, walk around the room, and roll cigarets and smoke until he had the next few lines, and so on until the end. He revised his poetry very little; the first drafts were usually the final ones.[19]

Whether or not Hovey followed this method in writing "Spring" is open to debate. If the report of one classmate is to be believed, the poem was written in a rather hurried manner.[20] Hovey, after landing in New York, had located some old college friends and had spent the night drinking beer with them. He told them that the plan of the poem was to have the first part about college life and the second part about the adult years. The two parts, preparation and action, were to be connected by a short lyric. In the poem, which begins in a lazy Walt Whitman-like manner, youth, the college years, and the period of preparation are all symbolized by spring:

> I said in my heart, "I am sick of four walls and a ceiling."
> I have need of the sky.
> I have business with the grass.
> I will up and get me away where the hawk is wheeling,
> Lone and high,
> And the slow clouds go by.
>
>   . . .
>
> I will get me away to the woods.
> Spring, like a huntsman's boy,
> Halloos along the hillsides and unhoods
> The falcon in my will.
> The dogwood calls me, and the sudden thrill
> That breaks in apple blooms down country roads
> Plucks me by the sleeve and nudges me away.
> The sap is in the boles today,
> And in my veins a pulse that yearns and goads."[21]

Arrived in the the woods, he falls under the hypnotic influence of
Spring, "With her gypsy ways"; and he knows it will not be long
before he joins the birds, bees, and flowers "on the old trail."

Then Hovey, no doubt remembering his recent night in New
York with his college friends, delivered his most famous words—
"The Stein Song." Spring has awakened in all men their desire for
fellowship, and they gather together to share their idealism, aspiration, and high spirits. The mood of the poem then shifts from the
dreamy lassitude of Whitman to the pulsing action of Kipling. From
the table where the goodfellows sing together is a road that runs
both east and west. "And the lure of the one is a roving quest,/ And
the lure of the other is a lotus dream." But, since it is really the same
road, a man will get to the same destination if he follows "the trail to
the end." There East and West become one like a man and woman
in marriage. The spring of the East takes the form of sap rising in a
tree; the Western spring is the free wings of a bird. But both springs
are really the one same spring—an urging upward.

The movement then shifts back to a rhymed free verse in which
the short line dominates. The effect is more lyrical and rapid than
that of the first part of the poem but is still not so bouncy as the
Kipling imitation. Hovey tries to convey the feeling of ecstasy that
comes with the rebirth of Nature:

> Spring in the heart!
> With her pinks and pearls and yellows!
> Spring, fellows,
> And we too feel the little green leaves a-start
> Across the bare-twigged winter of the mart.

He addresses the conventioneers and asks them to allow their youth
to return: "The campus is reborn in us today." They have not
gathered to discuss affairs of state or business matters as they do all
year long; they have come together to be boys again, for a "madcap
holiday."

The feeling of the natural spring is the base of the poem, but the
poet wonders if it is not symbolic of an even greater Spring
throughout the cosmos:

> For surely in the blind deep-buried roots
> Of all men's souls today
> A secret shiver shoots.

An underground compulsion of new birth
Lays hold upon the dark core of our being,
And unborn blossoms urge their uncomprehended way
Toward the outer day.
Unconscious, dumb, unseeing,
The darkness in us is aware
Of something potent burning through the earth,
Of something vital in the procreant air.

This feeling is not just the caprice of an idle brain: "Spring's not to be mistaken." Even dumb animals and flowers know when she arrives, and man is also assured by these dumb stirrings "of an impending something." There is a new ease, one in which all men will be comrades.

Man is aided in his quest for this ideal world by three great spirits: one free, one shackled, and one, though now free, halted by the effect of its former chain. The free spirit is Science, the wonder-worker, that can subdue "an alien world to man's desires." The chained spirit is Art which, if loosened, could take man by its imaginative powers into the heart of that alien world: "Till he shall live in it as in himself/ And know its longing as he knows his own." Religion comes behind; lame but serene and impenetrable, she is waiting her opportunity to yoke the other two spirits into action. For the time is coming when all bonds will be broken, and man will go forth free with the help of the spirits, "Rejoicing in the road he journeys on." It makes no difference which path he takes, East or West, for the goal is the same. His heart will leap high with the springtime, and he will not be discouraged by a late frost. Spring will come eventually: "For the ages fret not over a day/ And the greater tomorrow is on its way."

"Spring" is probably Hovey's best sustained effort; and, if the poem appears to be a mixture of rhythms and styles, it does so because it is really an ode. Hovey uses different styles to fit the several movements of the poem. For example, the free verse of Whitman—slow, quiet, and ponderous—is used for those passive movements of receiving truth; the quick moving meter of Kipling is used for occasions of action; and finally, Hovey's own lyrical free verse is used for the feelings of freedom and ecstasy. The poem shifts from style to style just as the human mind can shift from feeling to action to thought.

IV *Juvenilia*

Part four of *Along the Trail* contains, for the most part, poems
written early in Hovey's career; and this section begins with a long
poem subtitled "A Fantasy of the Washington Woodlands." This
work is really a fusing together of "The Faun" and several lyrics that
had appeared in *Vagabondia*, but it might originally have been
written as a long poem and then broken apart for poems in those
volumes. After this fantasy, short encomiums and eulogies appear
that are about artists and their work; college-student translations
from Greek and Latin; and at least one poem written before college.
This poem is a sonnet, "The South" (1880); it indicates the regional
influence of Sidney Lanier and is very good work for a sixteen-year-
old boy:

> Ah, where the hot wind with sweet odors laden
>   Across the roses faintly beats his wings,
>   Lifting a lure of subtle murmurings
>   Over the still pools that the herons wade in,
> Telling of some far sunset-bowered Aidenn,
>   And in an orange-tree an oriole sings,
>   Whereunder lies, dreaming of unknown things,
>   With orange-blossoms wreathed, a radiant maiden,—
> There is the poet's land, there would I lie
>   Under magnolia blooms and take no care,
>   And let my eyes grow languid and my mouth
> Glow with the kisses of the amorous air,
>   And breathe with every breath the luxury
>   Of the hot-cheeked, sweet, heavy-lidded South.[22]

In a short poem dated 1886, "August," the reader can see some of
Hovey's early Imagist ability in his attempt to describe a summer
seascape. The white heat of the August sun so bleaches all things
that the eye cannot distinguish between the sea and sky. Landward,
the trees keep their identity in a fashion similar to the way individual strength is nourished by religious faith. But the blue sky of
the western horizon is turned to a lead grey by the sun overhead.
The poem seems to be a comment about the sustaining powers that
individuals can find in religion:

> The white sky and the white sea run
> Their twin pearl-splendors into one,

> Nor can the eye distinguish these,
> Enchanted by the diableries
> The mist-witch conjures in the sun.
> Landward a white birch, like a nun,
> Whispers her leafy rosaries.
> Beyond, where the still woodland is,
> The blue west leadens into dun,
> Close to the dark tops of the trees.[23]

The poem "Angro-mainyus," written in 1888 while Hovey was still at the seminary, presents an insight into his theology. The poem is a study of the Persian religion, Zoroastrianism. The prophet Zoroaster had conceived the world as being governed by two principles: one was goodness and light and creativity; the other was evil and dark and destruction. In Hovey's poem, the evil principle is speaking, and he claims that he is the highest god and is wrathful and punishing:

> I am Angro-mainyus, the Most High God.
> Cry not unto me for mercy, for I am merciless.
> Sin and Death are my ministers,
> And my ways are ways of torture and the shedding of blood.
> I am the Lord thy God.
>
> I am the Destroyer.
> My sword is as fire in the forest;
> My feet are inexorable.
> Ask me not to deliver thee from evil.
> I am Evil.

Angro-mainyus admits that there is another god; Ahura-mazda, the kind one, the savior, who dwells in the sun while Angro-mainyus lives in the storm. But, though there are two thrones, the gods rule with one voice. There might be disagreement among their followers, but they are really the one and same god:

> The waves of the sea war mightily,
> But in the deeps there is calm.
> Ahura-mazda and I are one God;
> There is war between our legions,
> But in us peace.
> Behold, he knoweth my thoughts and I his,
> And there is no discord in us.

One of the gods works in the light; the other, in darkness. Their ways are different, but they are really two faces of the same God. Neither is superior to the other. Angro-mainyus is most insistent that he not be considered evil:

> But blaspheme not, calling me "Devil,"
> Neither saying, "There are two Gods";
> I am the Most High God,
> And I and Ahura-mazda are one.[24]

Hovey's poem owes a great deal to Ralph Waldo Emerson's "Brahma," supposedly a monologue by that god who is explaining how he is the reality behind everything. Hovey's poem also reflects Whitman's "Chanting the Square Deific" in which four different faces of the godhead, including the rebellious, are revealed. The significant point about Hovey's poem is that it is written from the viewpoint of the rebellious god, the dark one, the destroyer. Hovey believed that this god was as important and necessary as the other. In Zorastrianism, Angro-mainyus was to someday succumb to the good; but, in Hovey's theology, the dark is coequal with the light: they are both immortal and the same.

By having one God speak with two voices, Hovey tried to avoid the problems of dualism. In his attempt to solve the philosophical problems raised by Pantheism, he is again only partly successful. Pantheism is a theology that seeks to identify spiritual reality with the material universe. Besides leading to a confusing mixture of the spiritual and the material, Pantheism is hard pressed to come up with a creator for the world. Hovey insists that his God is a separate Creator; He is not the same as Nature. He is something more than the sum total of all natural phenomena. Although He is immanent in the world, He still exists beyond it, as Hovey establishes in "Transcendence":

> Though one with all that sense or soul can see,
> Not prisoned in his own creations he,
>   His life is more than stars or winds or angels—
> The sun doth not contain him nor the sea.[25]

But Hovey's God is not an aloof Creator; He is also the Divine Presence within the world as the quatrain "Immanence" indicates:

> Enthroned above the world although he sit,
> Still is the world in him and he in it;
>   The selfsame power in yonder sunset glows
> That kindled in the lords of Holy Writ.[26]

Hovey saw God's presence in the beauty of Nature and discovered Divine Will through natural events. Nature is the visible symbol of the transcendent God. In the concluding stanza of "The Laurel," Hovey attempts a sustained vision of God, describing His majesty, benevolence, and power. He also attempts to draw a line of demarcation between God and Nature:

> Behold, He is other than earth and transcendeth its seeming;
> Behold, He is one with the earth and the earth is His dreaming.
> Soul of the world, say the sage; yea, sooth, but not bound in a prison,
> For the soul dwelleth not in the body, but the body doth dwell in the
>   soul.[27]

God is perfection; men are but parts of the whole. Man's being consists in yearning to be united with Him. "O Lord, in Thee have we trusted; there is no life but in Thee!"

By establishing a God who transcends the natural world, Hovey attempts to escape the Pantheist dilemma—the ultimate identification of the material with the ideal. Nature, for Hovey, is important as a symbol; the material world is the means by which to ascend to spiritual reality. The climb does not have to be arduous or long; in fact, those scientific and analytic minds who spend time and energy dissecting and classifying Nature very likely miss the truth altogether. Hovey prefers the epistemological approach used by some Pantheists: the indirect, intuitive method—a process that is really no method at all but the absence of one. After the searcher ceases his striving, sloughs off his individuality, and becomes inert, truth flows into him.

This idea, which was developed by "The Faun" and several other poems in the *Vagabondia*, also appears in "The Messenger," who is the Angel of Death:

> Strong angel of the peace of God,
>   Not wholly undivined thy mien;
> Along the weary path I trod
>   Thou hast been with me though unseen.

My hopes have been a mad turmoil,
   A clutch and conflict all my life,
The very craft I loved a toil,
   And love itself a seed of strife.

But sometimes in a sudden hour
   I have been great with Godlike calm,
As if thy tranquil world of power
   Flowed in about me like a psalm.

And peace has fallen on my face,
   And stillness on my struggling breath;
And, living, I have known a space
   The hush and mastery of Death.

Stretch out thy hand upon me, thou
   Who comest as the still night comes!
I have not flinched at buffets; now
   Let Strife go by, with all his drums.[28]

A man who had not flinched at the buffets of fate was Henry
George, for he had fought to obtain a new economic order for
laborers and farmers. He influenced many Democratic politicians
with his ideas, and he had even entered the fray himself as candi-
date for mayor of New York. Many of George's ideas were sound,
but he was a man too advanced for the 1890's and was therefore
doomed to suffer continuous defeat. In his elegy to George, Hovey
asks that the ideals of the protector of the poor be remembered and
that the fight for equality and opportunity be continued.

Oh, he his death a clarion
To hearten, not dismay!
Fight on!
We have not lost the day.

. . .

Ay, if the day be lost, what then?
The cause, the cause endures.
Be men—
The triumph yet is yours,

The triumph every cause has won
That called men to be free!
Fight on,
Indomitable as he—

As he, our captain without stain,
The Bayard of the poor.
Be men!
Flinch no man in this hour.

Remember him that knew no fear,
And craved no diadem.
A cheer!
Be that his requiem.[29]

CHAPTER 6

Last Songs from Vagabondia

THE third volume of *Vagabondia*, which was assembled by Carman a few months after Hoovey's death, resembles in its appearance the previous two: the disc portrait on the cover and the illustrations on the endpapers are by Meteyard. This volume resembles the others in content, but the lyrics are a little longer and perhaps more somber. But the third collection is different in that it shows a Richard Hovey who had reached a poetic maturity during the last years of his life. His line has become much more disciplined and controlled; his imagery is sharper and more concrete; and, most important, intellectual substance, known as "meaning," is found behind many of his poems.

The volume opens with the song, "At the Crossroads," which is reminiscent of the earlier *Vagabondia*. In this paean about the heroic struggle against the overwhelming odds of the Establishment, the old themes of comradeship and adventure are present as is insistence upon the values of honesty, frankness, and fairness. The poem is held together by a thread of fatalism: the vagabonds know that they face almost certain defeat and are amazed whenever they win because the wheel of fortune is "always weighted" against them:

> You to the left and I to the right,
> For the ways of men must sever—
> And it well may be for a day and a night,
> And it well may be forever.
> But whether we meet or whether we part
> (For our ways are past our knowing),
> A pledge from the heart to its fellow heart
> On the ways we all are going!
> Here's luck!
> For we know not where we are going.

We have striven fair in love and war,
But the wheel was always weighted;
We have lost the prize that we struggled for,
We have won the prize that was fated.
We have met our loss with a smile and a song,
And our gains with a wink and a whistle,—
For, whether we're right or whether we're wrong,
There's a rose for every thistle.
Here's luck—
And a drop to wet your whistle!

Whether we win or whether we lose
With the hands that life is dealing,
It is not we nor the ways we choose.
But the fall of the cards that's sealing.
There's a fate in love and a fate in fight,
And the best of us all go under—
And whether we're wrong or whether we're right,
We win, sometimes, to our wonder.
Here's luck—
That we may not yet go under![1]

Although the theme of adventure is once more established in "At the Crossroads," that one of the greatest of adventures is a love affair is made clear in "Sea Sonnets." In an affair, especially if it be illicit or forbidden, two people are willing to forsake security and reputation in an attempt to satisfy some desire that goes beyond reason. It is a daring adventure to fall in love, an exploration, and a reaching out. That those in love are openly exposed to the buffets of fate is the theme developed in the "Sea Sonnets." When the close atmosphere of the harbor (society) stifles romance, the lovers cut their boat loose, push out into the dark, and take a voyage on an unknown sea—to which love is compared:

Out with the tide-afar, afar, afar,
Where will the wide dark take us, you and me—
The darkness and the tempest and the sea?
How long we waited where the tall ships are,
Disconsolate and safe within the bar!
Ocean forever calling us, but we—
God, how we stifled there, not dared be free
With a sharp knife and night and the wild dare!
But now, the hawser cut, adrift, away—

> Mad with escape, what care we to what doom
> The bitter night may bear us? Lost, alone,
> In a vague world of roaring surge astray,
> Out with the tide and into the unknown,
> Compassed about with rapture and the gloom![2]

The first sonnet sets the lovers adrift; the second emphasizes their precarious position. When they meet the storm, their light skiff is tossed about on the waves; and protection and warmth come from each other's arms. They have no sails, no star, and no port; they are helpless on the currents of fate. Yet, even though rebellious and lost, they have a joy that the great merchantmen with their valuable cargo can never know.

In the third sonnet the poet-lover speaks his fear. His every way seems blocked by some malicious destiny; formless monsters, "Dragons of Fate," feed laughingly upon his hope; but, in the end, he is saved by love. Love not only helps man break away from confining ports, the conformity and care of society; it also sustains the lover upon his adventure:

> Moon of my midlight! Moon of the dark sea,
> Where like a petrel's ghost my sleep is driven!
> Behold, about me and under and over me,
> The darkness and the waters and the heaven—
> Huge, shapeless monsters as of worlds in birth,
> Dragons of Fate, that hold me not in scope—
> Bar up my way with fierce, indifferent mirth,
> And fall in giant frolic on my hope.
> Their next mad rush may whelm me in the wave,
> The dreaded horror of the sightless deep—
> Only thy love, like moonlight, pours to save
> My soul from the despairs that lunge and leap.
> Moon of my night, though hell and death assail,
> The tremble of thy light is on my sail.[3]

Hovey's juncture of love and freedom helped to form a new pattern in American literature. Whenever the classic American authors wanted to free a character, they always sent him away from love and domesticity and toward the wilderness and nature; for love meant marriage, responsibility, and all the consequent frustrations of civilized life. Such entanglements James Fenimore Cooper's Natty Bumppo desperately avoided, and Nathaniel Hawthorne's independent Holgrave realizes in *The House of The Seven Gables* that his marriage to Phoebe will transform him from a creative to a conservative man. But Hovey's concept of daring love, especially when spiced with connotations of illicitness and impulsiveness, is different. Instead of entangling the individual with society, love helps to free him. Through love he breaks the chains of conformity, habit, and responsibility. If he is unhappy in his homelife, if he feels the pressures and cares of the work-a-day world, he need not despair and commit suicide; instead, he can try to escape the distress by having a love affair.

I *Here Comes the Navy*

Hovey continues the association of a sea journey with love in the long poem "Day and Night," the poem read at the Psi Upsilon convention held at Cornell in 1899. Like the poems written for previous fraternity occasions, it is an ode; and it features a combination of rhythms and meters and pivots around a lyric. "Day and Night" also resembles the other poems in emphasizing the themes of comradeship, adventure, and action. But in combination with these, Hovey joins another of his dominant themes: that there is need for a retreat into individuality, a period necessary for restoring the soul. Thus are "day" and "night" contrasted: day is the occasion for masculine comradeship in the struggle for eternal values; night offers the opportunity for feminine sensuality. Day and night are as opposite as action and reverie, as different as the worlds of reason and dream.

Then Hovey interjects in the last two stanzas the political idea about the need for Anglo-American unity. To Hovey, a time of peace could result from English-American domination of other nations; Anglo-Saxon law could bring justice and reason to the international scene; but peace would be possible only when it was forced by military and naval might:

Let us take up our work as a nation, the work of the day,
Clasp hands with our brothers of England—and who shall say nay?
And who shall say nay to our navies—the ships of us, sons of the Sea?
And who shall say nay to our Empires, to the Law that we set for the free?
But the best is the bond that's between us, the bond of the brothers in blood,

The bond of the men who keep silence, as the night when it falls on the
  flood,
As the night when it falls on the vastness, the splendour and lone of the
  wave,
The bond of the English forever, the bond of the free and the brave![4]

Hovey's pride in the American Navy reflects a rising sentiment of
the time. Before the Civil War, America was renowned for its sailing
prowess, largely because of the accomplishments of its whaling ships
and its Yankee Clippers. But after 1865, while other nations began
to build modern fleets, America turned to the development of
railways. Some people feared that the United States would not gain
a strong position in world affairs because it lacked a navy. In 1890
Admiral Alfred Mahan's book, *The Influence of Sea Power Upon
History*, persuaded many of the necessity of a strong navy, and the
United States began to acquire islands for coaling stations. Theodore
Roosevelt, as Under-Secretary of Navy, was instrumental in
modernizing the fleet; and the great victory of Admiral George
Dewey became a testimony to this insight.

"The Battle of Manila," which Hovey called a fragment, cele-
brates this victory of the Spanish-American War. He relates how the
American ships with daring navigation slipped past the fortress
Corregidor in the night and surprised the second Spanish Armada.
The Yankees were half-way around the world from home; with no
base nearby, they had either to win or to be captured. This out-
standing American victory told the world, says Hovey, that the
United States (together with England) now ruled the sea:

> By Cavite on the bay
> 'T was the Spanish squadron lay;
> And the red dawn was creeping
> O'er the city that lay sleeping
> To the east, like a bride, in the May.
> There was peace at Manila,
> In the May morn at Manila,—
>
> When ho, the Spanish admiral
> Awoke to find our line
> Had passed by gray Corregidor,
> Had laughed at shoal and mine,
> And flung to the sky its banners
> With "Remember" for a sign!

With the ships of Spain before
In the shelter of the shore,
And the forts on the right,
They drew forward to the fight,
And the first was the gallant Commodore;
In the doomed bay of Manila—
With succour half the world away,
No port beneath that sky,
With nothing but their ships and guns
And Yankee pluck to try,
They had left retreat behind them,
They had come to win or die!

For we spoke at Manila,
We said it at Manila,
Oh be ye brave, or be ye strong,
Ye build your ships in vain:
The children of the sea queen's brood
Will not give up the main:
We hold the sea against the world
As we held it against Spain.

Be warned by Manila,
Take warning by Manila,
Ye may trade by land, ye may fight by land.
Ye may hold the land in fee;
But go not down to the sea in ships
To battle with the free;
For England and America
Will keep and hold the sea![5]

Hovey actually seems to have been distressed by the peace. In war, the states had been united; but, after its end, each man went his own way, intent on personal gain. To Hovey in his poem "Peace," peace is really a pact with the Devil, a time for trade and corruption; people grow fat, venal, and selfish. Economics is worse than the "dismal science"; it is the "Devil's science." The real wealth of a country is not measured by commodities but by the character of its citizens, and it is impossible to estimate "honor" and "courage" by gold. While war is fearful and does bring great destruction, the death of the soul is far worse than the death of the body. True peace has to be won in battle; it does not come through cowardliness:

There is peace, you say. I believe you.
Peace? Ay, we know it well—
Not the peace of the smile of God, but the peace of the leer of Hell,
Peace, that the rich may fatten and barter their souls for gain,
Peace, that the hungry may slay and rob the corpse of the slain,
Peace, that the heart of the people may rot with a vile gangrene.
What though the men are bloodless! What's a man to a machine?
Here you come with your Economics. If ever the Devil designed
A science, 't was yours, I doubt not, a study to Hell's own mind,
Merciless, soulless, sordid, the science of selfish greed,
Blind to the light of wisdom, and deaf to the voice of need,
And you prate of the wealth of nations, as if it were bought and sold!
The wealth of nations is men, not silk and cotton and gold. . . . [6]

II   Amour Encore

Lyric poets who write of love soon become concerned with death,
for death is too absolute a rival for a lover to ignore: he does not even
need ruins to make him ruminate that someday death will take his
love away. So the happiness of love is vitiated by sadness, and
memories are all too painful. In the Petrarchan sonnet "A
Grotesque," Hovey has the morbid thought that, even though he
and his love will lie side by side in the damp earth some day, they
will be together no more. Above them will be their epitaphs—a
catalogue of their virtues, and a pious reference; and their only
immortality will be in supplying some antiquarian their names and
dates for a genealogical table:

> Our Gothic minds have gargoyle fancies.
>   Odd,
> That there will come a day when you and I
> Shall not be you and I, that we shall lie,
> We two, in the damp earth-mould, above each clod
> A drunken headstone in the neglected sod,
> Thereon the phrase, *Hic Jacet*, worn awry,
> And then our Virtues, bah!— and piety—
> Perhaps some cheeky reference to God!
> And haply after many a century
> Some spectacled old man shall drive the birds
> A moment from their song in the lonely spot
> And make a copy of the quaint old words—
> They will then be quaint and old—and all for what?
> To fill a gap in a genealogy. [7]

Since even temporary separations are painful for a lover, the poet tells his loved one how he misses her—her look, her walk, her exciting talk—in his sonnet "At a Summer Resort." The people at the boardinghouse bore him, and the beauty of nature cannot arouse him as it did before. He lives only for night when he can imagine her in his presence again:

> I miss you so by day, your look, your walk,
> The rustle of your draperies on the stair,
> Our Leyden-jar-fuls of electric talk,
> The sense of you about me everywhere.
> The people bore me in the boarding-house,
> I hardly can accord them yes or no;
> The beauty of the valleys can arouse
> No such elation as a year ago.
> But when the last dull guest has gone to bed
> And only crickets keep me company,
> In the mesmeric night when truth is said—
> When you, dear loveliness with drooping eye,
> Demurely enter through the unreal wall,
> And I forget you went away at all.[8]

In "Japanese Love-Song," the condensed imagery seems to indicate that Hovey had some knowledge about Oriental poetry. The images are fused together somewhat in the manner of the Japanese *haiku*, but no indication exists as to where Hovey might have gained this knowledge. Perhaps he came across a translation of Oriental poetry in a Paris book stall; maybe he met an Eastern scholar at Columbia; and perhaps the stylistic similarities of the short lines and unexplicated images are only accidental.

> How you start away!
> —As a flame starts from a gust.
> Flame-heart o' the dust!
> Sudden startle of dismay!
> Swift triumph in distrust!
>
> Flash and tremble of escape,
> Fierce with desire!
> Rippled water shot with fire
> Wary of the rape
> Of the eyes that sire!

Radiant no-and-yes!
Deer-flight and panther-thirst!
Blest and accurst!
Sword-splendour past the guess
Of Heaven's best and Hell's worst!

So you sprang up from yourself,
Burnt to supremacies,
Star-demoned by a kiss—
Night turned fire-elf,—
Wonder and all amiss![9]

In "Ornithology," a poem that describes the love antics of two sparrows, the hen is playing the coquette, teasing and flirting with her pursuer. After a while, he tires of the chase and looks for a less reluctant mate; and the lesson for women is obvious. While the poem might not be an accurate analysis of bird behavior, it does make a good fable. Its message, however, is not so important as its style. The verse is not entirely free: the line is irregular, but the rhythm is definite iambic. There is no stanzaic arrangement, but Hovey does group the thoughts into paragraphs. The lines are rhymed, but the rhymes are allowed to fall naturally and therefore be more exciting because of their unexpectedness. But the best stylistic device is the poetic sentence that Hovey uses: long, sustained, flowing lines alternate with short quick bursts; and both seem to capture the actual movements of the birds. The sound communicates the sense of flit and flight:

SWEETHEART, do you see up yonder through the leaves
The elm tree interweaves,
How that cock-sparrow chases his brown mate?
Look, where she perches now
Upon the bough
And turns her head to see if he pursue her,
Half frightened, half elate
To have so bold and beautiful a wooer.
See, he alights beside her. How his wings
Quiver with amorous passionings!
How voluble their chattering courtship is!
Soon will he know
Love's joys in overflow,
Love's extreme ecstasies.

No, off she flies!
Just as she seemed about to be subdued
To his impetuous desire!
How angrily he scolds, with wicked eyes
Following her flight, and turns his tiny ire
Against the innocent tree and pecks the wood!
While she—ah, the coquette!—
Lurks yonder in the cleft where the great tree
Breaks into boughs, and peeps about to see
If he is coming yet.
She's in for a game of lovers' hide-and-seek,
And longs to have him find the hiding-place,
Although she feigns concealment, so to pique
His passion to a chase.

In vain—he will not look
For all her sweet allurements. Out she whisks
Demurely from her nook,
As if she did not see and were not seen,
And perks herself and frisks
Her delicate tail as a lady flirts her fan.
And now slips back again to her retreat
And waits for one hushed moment in serene
Unfluttered expectation that the plan
Have issue sweet.
What, will he not come yet?
See how she glances at him unawares,
Tosses her head and gives herself high airs
In such a pretty pet.

Cruel! he turns away,
Affecting unconcern.
All those endearing wiles are wrought in vain.
Alas, unlucky flirt! too late you learn
That long delays will make the eagerest lover
Aweary of pursuing. Nay,
Too late you fly half way to him again.
You will not so recover
The passion that you played with. Off he flies
And now is lost in the thick shade
Of lilac bushes further down the glade.
Another mistress charms his amorous eyes.
Have a care, sweetheart, or as he some day
I too will fly away.[10]

"Her Valentine" is an amusing piece that is as relevant in 1970 as
it was in 1900. since the poem was written for a "new woman."
Hovey cannot send her a valentine or his chances would be ruined
forever; she would not believe in such romantic trinkets. In fact, she
shuns romance, fearing her loss of freedom in marriage. She prefers
to stand on the L-train rather than accept a seat from a gentleman;
she paints pictures, writes books, and can earn her own way; and
she is an advocate of dress reform. She will attempt anything—
athletics, politics, professions—but the poet is content to let her
have her own way. If he does, he will eventually win her.

WHAT, send her a valentine? Never!
I see you don't know who "she" is.
I should ruin my chances forever;
My hopes would collapse with a fizz.

I can't see why she scents such disaster
When I take heart to venture a word;
I've no dream of becoming her master,
I've no notion of being her lord.

All I want is to just be her lover!
She's the most up-to-date of her sex,
And there's such a multitude of her,
No wonder they call her complex.

She's a bachelor, even when married,
She's a vagabond, even when housed;
And if ever her citadel's carried
Her suspicions must not be aroused.

She's erratic, impulsive and human,
And she blunders,—as goddesses can;
But if she's what they call the New Woman,
Then I'd like to be the New Man.

I'm glad she makes books and paints pictures,
And typewrites and hoes her own row,
And it's quite beyond reach of conjectures
How much further she's going to go.

When she scorns, in the L-road, my proffer
Of a seat and hangs on to a strap;
I admire her so much, I could offer
To let her ride up on my lap.

Let her undo the stays of the ages,
That have cramped and confined her so long!
Let her burst through the frail candy cages
That fooled her to think they were strong!

She may take me off, for example,
And she probably does when I'm gone.
I'm aware the occasion is ample;
That's why I often take on.

I'm so glad she can win her own dollars
And know all the freedom it brings.
I love her in shirt-waists and collars,
I love her in dress-reform things.

I love her in bicycle skirtlings—
Especially when there's a breeze—
I love her in crinklings and quirklings
And anything else that you please.

I dote on her even in bloomers—
If Parisian enough in their style—
In fact, she may choose her costumers,
Wherever her fancy beguile.

She may lecture (all lectures but curtain),
Make money, and naturally spend,
If I let her have her way, I'm certain
She'll let me have mine in the end![11]

III   *Truth and Poetry*

A few of the poems in *Last Songs* reflect Hovey's concern about
the relationship between truth and poetry, but he does not try to
argue that the poet expresses truth in the form of occasional moral or
psychological insights. That sort of revelation would be knowledge,
a particular or separate variety of truth; and it would be no different
from the observations of scientists or historians. Moreover, this type
of knowledge is not truth for Hovey since ultimate truth is not to be
found singly; it is discovered only in the total harmonious arrangement of things. This harmony the poet perceives better than
the scientist or philosopher, for Hovey agrees with Keats that
beauty is truth. In Hovey's poem "Harmonics," he explains the
poet's view of truth and the creation of "the whole" of that truth:

Truth is not a creed,
For it does not need
Ever an apology.
Truth is not an ology;
'T is not part, but all.
Priests and savants shall
Never solve the mystic
Problem. The artistic
Mind alone of all can tell
What is Truth.

"Poet, thou art wisest;
Dogmas thou despisest—
Science little prizest.
Tell us, for thou knowest well,
What is truth."

Spake the seekers to an holy
Bard, who answered, mild and lowly—
This, all this, was in the olden
Days when Saturn's reign was golden—
"Shall I read the riddle—
Tell you what is Truth?
Truth is not the first
Not the last or middle;
'T is the beautiful
And symmetric whole,
Embracing best and worst,
Embracing age and youth.

"All the universe
Is one mighty song,
Wherein every star
Chants out loud and strong
Each set note and word
It must aye rehearse.
Though the parts may jar,
The whole is as one chord."[12]

Hovey was convinced that there was a benevolent idealistic arrangement of things and he believed that poetry was the best medium for communicating the divine structure. The will of God was behind the beauty of the natural world, and the poet's sacred obligation was to reveal the intent of God to man. The poet's tool was language: "In the beginning was the Word." As Hovey makes clear in "The Gift of Art," no understanding or acceptance of God on the part of the people could exist without language; the poet was necessary for maintaining social order.

> I Dreamed that a child was born; and at his birth
> The Angel of the Word stood by the hearth
> And spake to her that bare him: "Look without!
> Behold the beauty of the Day, the shout
> Of colour to glad colour, rocks and trees
> And sun and sea and wind and sky! All these
> Are God's expression, art-work of his hand,
> Which men must love ere they may understand,
> By which alone he speaks till they have grace
> To hear his voice and look upon his face.
> For first and last of all things in the heart
> Of God as man the glory is of art.
> What gift could God bestow or man beseech,
> Save spirit unto spirit uttered speech?
> Wisdom were not, for God himself could find
> No way to reach the unresponsive mind,
> Sweet Love were dead, and all the crowded skies
> A loneliness and not a Paradise.
> Teach the child language, mother. . . ."[13]

From a vantage point on a cliff, Hovey, surveying plain and hills and sky, once felt the divine breath of God. It was an inspiration (meaning, "to breathe in") no doubt similar to that felt by poets of the past—Sappho, Pindar, and Dante. Hovey might also have named Wordsworth, for the idea of the poem "From the Cliff" seems somewhat similar to "Tintern Abbey" because of the impressionistic natural view from a summit.

> Here on this ledge, the broad plain stretched below,
> The calm hills smiling in immortal mirth,
> The blue sky whitening as it nears the earth,
> Afar where all the summits are aglow,
> I feel a mighty wind upon me blow
> Like God's breath kindling in my soul a birth
> Of turbulent music struggling to break girth
> I pass with Dante through eternal woe,
> Quiver with Sappho's passion at my heart,
> See Pindar's chariots flashing past the goal,
> Triumph o'er splendours of unutterable light

> And know supremely this, O God,—Thou art,
> Feeling in all this tumult of my soul
> Grand kinship with the glory of Thy might.[14]

Although Wordsworth usually received his inspiration from nature, he did admit in his sonnet, "London 1802," that "Earth has not anything to show more fair" since the collective heart of the city seemed somehow to symbolize the Supreme Being. In "New York," a sonnet that might be a negative reply to Wordsworth, Hovey relates the depressing aspects of a large city. The depression is found not so much in the soot and grime as in the heartbreak, despair, and sad anonymity of so many people who are crowded together:

> The low line of the walls that lie outspread
> Miles on long miles, the fog and smoke and slime,
> The wharves and ships with flags of every clime,
> The domes and steeples rising overhead!
> It is not these. Rather it is the tread
> Of the million heavy feet that keep sad time
> To heavy thoughts, the want that mothers crime,
> The weary toiling for a bitter bread,
> The perishing of poets for renown,
> The shriek of shame from the concealing waves,
> Ah, me! how many heart-beats day by day
> Go to make up the life of the vast town!
> O myriad dead in unremembered graves!
> O torrent of the living down Broadway![15]

"The Adventurers," the last poem of *Last Songs*, brings the three volumes of *Vagabondia* to a fitting conclusion. Written jointly by Carman and Hovey (although the latter's style is dominant), this poem is about the vagabonds who have appeared throughout history as both soldiers of fortune and prophets of hope. Outcasts they are, sons of Ishmael, or so they appear to be since they have no position in temporal society. But they serve a king and government greater than any on earth, for they are the true messengers of God's will. Their exploration is of the soul; their message is the power of love:

> We are adventurers who come
> Before the merchants and the priests;
> Our only legacy from home,
> A wisdom older than the East's.

Soldiers of Fortune, we unfurl
The banners of a forlorn hope,
Leaving the city smoke to curl
O'er dingy roofs where puppets mope.

We are the Ishmaelites of earth
Who at the crossroads beat the drum;
None guess our lineage nor our birth,
The flag we serve nor whence we come.

We claim a Sire that no man knows,
The emperor of Nights and Days,
Who saith to Caesar, "Go,"—he goes,
To Alexander, "Stay,"—he stays.

Out of a greater town than Tyre,
We march to conquer and control
The golden hill-lands of Desire,
The Nicaraguas of the soul.

We have cast in our lot with Truth;
We will not flinch nor stay the hand,
Till on the last skyline of youth
We look down on his fair new land.

We put from port without a fear,
For Freedom on this Spanish Main;
And the great wind that bore us here
Will drive our galleys home again.

If not, we can lie down and die,
Content to perish with our peers,
So one more rood we gained thereby
For Love's Dominion through the years.[16]

CHAPTER 7

To the End of the Trail

RICHARD Hovey's last book, *To the End of the Trail* (1908), was edited by his wife and appeared eight years after his death. Like *The End of the Trail*, it is an anthology that contains some of his earliest verse with some of his latest, translations from French, previously published works, and fragments. It begins with three long poems—"The Laurel," "Seaward," and "A Vision of Parnassus"—that are concerned with poetry and poets. "The Laurel," written for Mrs. Sidney Lanier, had been privately printed and circulated among friends; but Hovey, who had never published it, was holding it back for a projected volume of "Odes and Hymns" which never materialized.

The "Laurel" theme of poetic beauty versus materialism is repeated in "A Vision of Parnassus," which had served as the dedication for *Launcelot and Guenevere*. In this poem which is a travesty of a Medieval romance, the poet acts the role of the knight, and the material corruptions of modern society are the dragons and beasts that threaten beauty. "A Vision" begins with an invocation to God, the Creator, and to Apollo, the God of Poetry. Few worship at Apollo's shrine these days, but the altars of Astarte (lust) and Mammon (greed) are busy. The poet relates how, while musing on Apollo's Parnassus, he sees a beautiful lady running, chased by a horrid hound. When he attempts to save her, he is warned by a stranger that the beast cannot be overcome by a mortal arm; other weapons must be forged to destroy him.

The speaker, who turns out to be Shakespeare, leads Hovey farther up the hill where they encounter Dante, Aeschylus, Homer, David, and Goethe. Shakespeare tells Hovey about the lady and the hound—the destruction of beauty by materialism:

> This is that lady whom I throned so high!
> Alas, that she should be brought down so low!

> Each morning from that horror she must fly,
> Each morning be devoured by that fell foe;
> Yet ever when the new day quickenth,
> Again she must renew her ancient woe—
> Perpetual struggle and perpetual death![1]

If the young poet (Hovey) will be her knight, he will find foes in
every tree (the critics) who will shoot venomed arrows at him; and
the magic sword necessary to destroy this monster lies on the altar
in Apollo's temple. When Hovey raises doubts about his ability to
perform these heroic deeds, the bards encourage him. Those who
think Hovey audacious in classing himself with the greatest poets of
antiquity miss the point. His intent was not to equate himself with
the immortals but to show that he was the heir of their eternal flame
and that his duty was to keep the great tradition alive.

Hovey had much to say about the life and rewards of the poet in
"Seaward, an Elegy on the Death of Thomas William Parsons."
Even though Parsons was much older and wrote classical and re-
strained verse, Hovey had warm regard for him. Parson's life
seemed to document the struggle of all poets for recognition and
acceptance. Indeed, there must have been something about him
that suggested the ideal poet because he was the model for Henry
Wadsworth Longfellow's poet in *Tales of a Wayside Inn.*

Hovey was spending the summer by the sea in Nova Scotia when
he learned of Parson's death, and he responded with an immediate
elegy, written in modified rhyme royal. The poem opens with
imagery reminiscent of Sidney Lanier's "The Marshes of Glynn."
Hovey, standing upon the yellow marshes, hears the roar of the sea
beyond the dunes:

> I know that there the tide is coming in,
>   Secret and slow, for in my heart I feel
> The silent swelling of a stress akin;
>   And in my vision, lo! blue glimpses steal
> Across the yellow marsh-grass, where the flood,
>   Filling the empty channels, lifts the keel
> Of one lone catboat bedded in the mud.[2]

The sea provides the controlling imagery of the poem and key-
notes the mood, but it is also symbolic. It represents the creative
source of all life, the life-force that permeates the world just as the

sea threads the marshes. As Hovey watches the tide come in, the
visual world begins to change. Suddenly, Parsons is at his side,
"Song's gentle, shy recluse":

> The hermit thrush of singers, few might draw
> So near his ambush in the solitude
> As to be witness of the holy awe
> And passionate sweetness of his singing mood.
> Not oft he sang, and then in ways apart,
> Where foppish ignorance might not intrude
> To mar the joy of his sufficing art.

The poem then begins to follow the step of the classical elegy. There
is use of the pathetic fallacy: the crying of the surf is echoed by the
dirge of the seashell and by the mourning of the marshes and the
dunes. Viking Death is blamed for his rapacity. Then begins the
procession of the mourners, the popular poets of the day: Joaquin
Miller; James Whitcomb Riley; Amelie Rives, "Virginia's hawk of
song."

The mood and the imagery of the poem change about half way.
After the grief comes calm vision, and the poet asks why men should
be frightened by shadows. The marshes reflect a "golden joy"; the
sea "Shouts to the sun and leaps in radiant spray"; the breakers
cease to mourn and begin to play laughingly along the shore. Death
is no longer personified as a pirate; it is now a skillful ship captain.
The deceased will have a safe journey to paradise where Parsons will
be welcomed by his "high compeers": Longfellow; Poe; William
Cullen Bryant; Emerson "of the antique zest/And modern vision";
Lowell; and Whitman "with the old superb aplomb." Now Parsons
will receive his reward of immortality for his service to God and his
dedication to the supreme values. The poem wells into a Whitman-
like praise of death, but it then returns to the reflective mood of the
beginning.

Hovey awakes from his vision of immortality and returns to the
reality of the marshes. But his perception has changed. Before, he
had been confined to the immediate reality of marsh and tide; now,
his sight has stretched to the rim of the sea. The lone catboat
embedded in the mud at the beginning has been freed by the tide,
and white ships are bound for ports all over the world:

> Some bound for Flemish ports or Genovese,
> Some for Bermuda bound, or Baltimore;

Others, perchance, for further Orient seas,
Sumatra and the straits of Singapore,
Or antique cities of remote Cathay,
Or past Gibraltar and the Libyan shore
Through Bab-el mandeb eastward to Bombay;

And one shall signal flaming Teneriffe,
And the Great Captive's ocean-prison speak,
Then on beyond the demon-haunted cliff,
By Madagascar's palms and Mozambique.
Till in some sudden tropic dawn afar
The Sultan sees the colors at her peak
Salute the minarets of Zanzibar.

I *Symbolism Defined*

The poems written toward the end of Hovey's life show increasing indebtedness to the Symbolist movement. He seemed more concerned with creating concrete specific images; and, in some of the poems, as in the fragment below, "A Stéphane Mallarmé," meaning was sacrificed for the sake of pure imagery:

On battlemented Morningside
The gold alembic days distil,
The violet rocks remember yet
The winter winds that moaned and sighed
The grasses and the leaves are still.[3]

To the End of the Trail contains one of Hovey's major contributions to the Symbolist movement: translations of ten of Maeterlinck's poems, three of Mallarmé's, and one of Verlaine's. His other significant contribution had been his essay, "Modern Symbolism and Maurice Maeterlinck," which begins with the statement that all language is symbolic and all art is language. The artist uses the subject matter of the material world to express his spiritual thoughts and feelings. Mankind may be classified into three epistemological classes: those who see only the thing; those who see mainly the idea behind the thing: and those who have a tendency to personify all experience—to give human characteristics to inanimate things.

The first class represents the natural mind; the second, the ethical; and the third, the poetic. None of these operates to the exclusion of the others. If the thing is dominant in the artist's mind, then the output will be realistic; if the abstract idea is his primary concern, then the art produced will be symbolic; if the soul dominates, a poetic effort is the result. The physical body speaks for itself, and emotions have their own spontaneous language; but, to communicate an idea, some representation must be created: "The life and the heart find utterance through natural correspondences,—metaphors that exist by the constitution of things; but for the mental we must find artificial correspondences, allegories, and consciously invented symbols."[4]

The difference between modern and past symbolism is that the latter was mainly allegory. Modern symbolism communicates through implication rather than definite statement: "The story, whether romantic . . . or realistic . . . lives for itself and produces no impression of being a masquerade of moralities; but behind every incident, almost behind every phrase, one is aware of a lurking universality." Symbolism, unlike allegory, shows no trace of being made to order: "Instead of looking at marionettes with the most gross and palpable strings, we see a living picture, with actuality and motive sufficient to itself." Modern symbolism, says Hovey, is a spontaneous and an independent movement that consists of many different writers from different cultures. The work of Canadian poets, such as Carman, is different from the French school in that it is "saner, fresher, and less morbid. The clear air of the lakes and prairies of Canada blows through it. It has not the kind of likeness that comes of imitation." Symbolism, then, is not so much a school as a drift in art that results in a type of poetry that appeals more to the imagination and the emotions than to the intellect.

When Hovey made other comments about Symbolism a few years later in an interview, he said that there was no school as such but that the poets had several similarities. They believed in a "root-and-branch democracy," in the independence of women, in the virility of verse, in the Hellenic attitude of joy, in philosophic idealism, in the use of religious themes, and in greater freedom of technique. In commenting upon technique, he added that the new poets were attracted by the "flexibility, complexity, and naturalness of *vers libre*. The new poets do not desire to do away with the old forms: their aim is enrichment, not impoverishment. They believe that the purpose of the form is to reveal the spirit"[5]—or, as architect Louis Sullivan had observed a few years earlier, "form follows function."

Some of Hovey's statements about the beliefs, techniques, and characteristics of Symbolists appear quite ironic today after seventy years of Symbolism, for the reader does not find too many democratic sentiments in Ezra Pound's verse, nor is T. S. Eliot's work thought to be virile. Hovey, of course, was not able to foretell what course the movement would follow, but he, at least, among the American poets of the time was aware of Symbolism; he knew that it would have great impact; and he helped inject the French strain into American literature and thereby cure our poetry of inbred provincialism. Although Hovey was incorrect about a few of the minor points of the movement, history seems to have proved his major thesis true. He believed that the one common bond the Symbolists had was their belief in individuality: "the conception of the human being as something apart from the rest of the world rather than the conception of him as merely one of the mass."[6] This concern for individuality is a dominant one of contemporary poets; and, if there is disillusionment and melancholy in their work instead of joy, it is because the power structure of the modern world has robbed man of his opportunities for individuality.

II *Flowers of Evil*

Hovey made several indirect comments about literature in a series of sonnets addressed to Victorian poets: Dante Gabriel Rossetti, Algernon Swinburne, and Matthew Arnold. In these poems he indicated how close he was to the Esthetic writers and to their attempt to remove moral judgments from literature. In "Dante Gabriel Rossetti," Hovey praised that poet for keeping his thought pure and for maintaining his "high sorrowing position." Swinburne is compared in "To Swinburne—I" to a "faery" king who lives in an enchanted garden in which he often walks and bends to listen to hollow murmurs or to scent a subtile perfume: pleasures that none but he and the spiritual wind can know. In another sonnet, "To Swinburne—II," Swinburne is pictured as living among pristine nature with the powers that rule: "Sea, wind, and sun, the gods who rule the earth." Swinburne and Rossetti may have been aloof from their age and withdrawn, but they never surrendered their dedication to art.

However, the role of Matthew Arnold was different. He had a poet within him but was too faint-hearted to withstand the pressures and demands of the middle-class Philistines who dominated his time. To

get peace, he sacrificed his inner passion; and the poet within him
was slain. Arnold's participation with his era was wrong because he
made poetry a servant to society's demands:

> There was a poet in him. But his art
> Grew too faint hearted to withstand the strain
> And turmoil of the age. He sought to gain
> Peace only, all the passion of his heart
> He slew, that, a little space apart
> For quiet of his soul he might attain;
> And so the poet in him fell self-slain,
> Sang its own swan-song and was not. O heart!
> He has found a deeper peace than he pursued
> And his worn eyes at last behold the ways
> That open for man's limitless up-leaping;
> And God's voice softly wakes his poethood
> Anew, as the Master bent of old to raise
> The dust that loved him, saying: "Not dead, but sleeping."[7]

   Although Hovey agreed with the poets of the Esthetic school that
art ought to satisfy the requirements of beauty before morality,
there was one very fundamental difference between him and them.
Estheticism was largely an anti–middle-class movement, and it
seemed to be as concerned with ridiculing conventional morality
and opinion as the professional middle-class moralists were with
censoring the Esthetic Bohemian behavior. The Esthetics liked to
shock; they frequently used decadent themes just to disturb the
bourgeois conscience. Hovey used such subject matter for different
reasons: decadence was a part of life, and he wished to exclude
nothing. Hovey's art had a democratic base: like Walt Whitman, he
was more interested in including all existence and experience within
the framework of literature than in condemning any particular
segment of it.
   Hovey did not hesitate to treat subjects, whether degenerate or
wholesome. In a sonnet, "To Prof. C. F. Richardson," dedicated to
his teacher, Hovey states that his poems will be gay and ghastly,
merry and sad, trivial and tragic; for so he found life to be. Good and
evil are woven in such an inextricable pattern that no man can
discriminate between them, and only God can judge:

> Such as the seashore gathers from the sea—
> Shells whose glad opal sunlight makes more glad,

And dead men's bones by bitter seaweed clad—
Teacher and friend, these songs I send to thee.
Gay things and ghastly mingled, seem to me
Here are alike; the merry and the sad,
The trivial and tragic, good and bad,
For so I find the ways of life to be.
Evil and good are woven upon the loom
Of fate in such inextricable wise
That no man may be bold to judge and say,
"This thing is good, that evil," till the day
When God shall blazon on regenerate skies
The justice of His pardon and His doom. [8]

III *"Don Juan"*

Although much of Hovey's poetry reflects a deep-grained patriotism, his acceptance of America still remains somewhat ambivalent. Like many another author, he seemed to love America better than he liked it; that is, he preferred the idea of democracy to its real existence. He criticized his countrymen's materialism, false values, and pretensions in many poems but perhaps most effectively in "Don Juan." In this poem of some four hundred lines, Hovey pretends to be Lord Byron who is speaking after death. Hovey's poem is written in the same ottava rima stanza as Byron's masterpiece, in the same conversational style, and with similar outrageous rhymes. Hovey's imitation is even more meandering than the original since the poet's thin plot line is used for comments about life, letters, and love. The mock-mock-epic begins with Juan's standing on the deck of a ship that is returning to America from Europe. He has been admiring the brillance and glory of the stars, and this majestic order of the heavens has filled him with beauty and serenity. When he sees a new star rise in the sky, he wonders to what constellation it belongs;

And then a fellow-passenger strolls up and says:
"That's Fire Island. Well, the trip was short.
To-morrow we shall be at Del's to sup.
I wonder whether Dewey is in port.
And Lipton—do you think he'll lift the cup?
Thank Fortune, we'll have news soon of some sort.
I've such a next-day's thirst for information,
I'd even be content to read *The Nation.*

"Do you think war's declared on the Boers yet? . . ."
And Juan sighed and wished it were—internally—
And all his dreams dropped with his cigarette
O'er the ship's side. He was bored infernally.[9]

The fellow passenger turns out to be a millionaire who, though
widely travelled (once to Japan in his own yacht), is still completely
conventional. His name is Smythe (it had once been Smith), and he
has inherited his wealth. He knows good living—rich dinners and
fine wines. Though he possesses everything money can buy, he
really owns nothing—not his Oriental rugs nor his Chippendale
furniture, his works of art, his ideas, his houses, his horses, and,
least of all, his wife:

She was a slight, red-headed type,
With eyes like sealskin and a cheek like ermine.
Soft, lush, and deep; her lips were overripe,
If anything—but who would dare determine?
She fenced, rode, flirted, smoked—had hit the pipe,
They say—(but all looked dainty in her mien)—
For Ellinor (her Christian name was Ellinor)
Had twenty-seven different kinds of hell in her.[10]

The mention of hell occasions a long discussion of morality.
Hovey-Byron claims that his purpose is moral although his methods
might not appear to be. A man can be both jolly and virtuous; on the
other hand, a grave exterior often masks a lecherous mind. Then the
discussion returns to Ellinor, the new woman who is bold and daring in both spirit and dress:

Born a roamer
She found escape of soul in being shocking.
Witty she was, and wicked; knew her Omar,
Browning and Kipling,—yet was no blue-stocking.[11]

Her apparent wickedness is not really evil because it does not arise
from malice. Her risqué manner exasperates good women because
they cannot compete with it. Yet she is serious under her frivolity,
and a mild restraint governs her maddest moods which "Gave to her
merriment a patrician quality/ As far from 'sportiness' as from con-
straint." She would have tempted even St. Anthony, the first monk:

> Well, I'm not Anthony—thank God for that!
> Though he's in Heaven, and I'm—where I expected.
> He's sitting with the angels, singing flat;
> And I'm in hell, and not half so dejected
> As you'd suppose, considering "where I'm at."
> I'm rather glad that I was not elected
> And foreordained to Heaven before earth's testing,
> I find that hell's so much more interesting.[12]

The poet reminds the reader that he (Byron) had promised in the First Canto that the poem would be as epic as he could make it, which means, of course, that he would create an episode in Hell. He can keep his promise now even better than he intended because he can write from firsthand experience. The reader should not be disappointed if Hell is not like Dante or Homer pictured it, for it has been modernized.

Byron tells how he came to Hell. After he had died in Greece, his soul was fought over by two angels: "One was a Shape of Light,/ superb and cold,/ And one of Darkness, passionate and imperial." Each was beautiful—and female; and he liked both. His good angel, something of a prude, was so displeased by his lack of discrimination that she returned to Heaven and left him alone with the evil angel. In such a manner was his damnation settled.

When he got to Hell, he found that, though the outside was drab and sinister as pictured in the old books, the inside was up-to-date. Lath and plaster covered the grim stones, and the walls were decorated with prints from Renaissance artists—even from the Sistine Chapel. There were Turkish baths, dormitories, gymnasiums, and laboratories. All the devils were going to school, and they were led by Lucifer "with spectacles on brow." They apologized for the primitive ways of old and practiced modern criminology instead. The whole place was one vast reformatory that has more interest than Heaven:

> Still it is interesting here because
> There are such interesting people—lots!
> Caesar, Petronius, Attila, Morgause,
> Nell Gwynne, Aspasia, Mary Queen of Scots,
> And more good company that I can pause
> To mention, have their numbers, and their cots,
> And Heaven is much more boresome, so they say,—
> A sort of middle-class Y.M.C.A.[13]

The inmates are all photographed, numbered, and measured. There are no punishments except those, which, Mikado-like, match the crime. For example, Midas continues to heap useless gain; "Napoleon still leads armies—to his ruin"; and Byron continues to write *Don Juan.*

Although the world is not missing great literature because Hovey failed to extend the mock-epic, the historian wishes that he had. Hovey, who had a gift for satire and a large experience, could have made comments about the political, social, and literary life of his era that could have been most revealing. As Hovey's work stands, the reader can be thankful for his sketches of the dull, conventional American millionaire and his exciting, not-so-conventional wife.

Moreover, Hovey's "Don Juan" offers his most explicit criticism of American life. The same criticism that is implied in the Vagabond poems and in the college songs becomes overt in "Don Juan," and Hovey answers those "jingoes" and others who shout cant and platitudes about American freedom and opportunity:

> That land is free where the inhabitants
> Are free; the rest is merely oratory.
> The trouble is that human history grants
> No glimpse of such a land in all its story.
> One slavery dies but by another's lance;
> And in the process many men get glory,
> But the vast millions only fresh disasters—
> Monarchs or mobs—it is but a change of masters.[14]

To Hovey, other serfdoms exist besides feudalism, for a man's liberty may be measured by the source of his income. To some observers, American economic life after the Civil War was really a form of feudalism. The worker was the hapless serf whose very existence depended upon the whim and caprice of the industrialists, often known as the "king" or the "monarch" of some commodity, or as a "robber baron" whose armed horse was the railroad. Freedom, argued Hovey, was an illusion:

> Muscle was King once; now the King is money.
> The form of government—the world's partition—
> Those things are but the wax and not the honey;
> "The means whereby I live" is the condition
> Of Freedom as of life. It is not funny

> To eat but by the other man's permission;
> And it makes little difference to the stoker
> If Thomas Platt be Lord or Richard Croker*.[15]

*Platt was the Republican boss of New York, and Croker, the boss of
Tammany Hall.

IV *Modern Love*

To the End of the Trail concludes with nine sonnets, eight English and one French, that were written for Hovey's wife, the Marna
of his poems. The dominant theme of this cycle is the degree of trust
and fidelity that ought to exist in modern love which might possess
very little of either quality, says Hovey. The loved one should not
trust the words of his poems for he can write to any slut as well as he
can to her. There will be infidelity and betrayal on both sides. A
single standard should prevail in love, and a woman owns the same
philandering rights as a man. If she does transgress, he will have to
forgive her; for, like Gawaine in Hovey's "The Last Love of
Gawaine," his own record is hardly spotless.

> You will betray me—oh, deny it not!
> What right have I, alas, to say you nay?
> I traitor of ten loves, what shall I say
> To plead with you that I be not forgot?
> My love has not been squandered jot by jot
> In little loves that perish with the day.
> My treason has been ever to the sway
> Of queens; my faith has known no petty blot.
> You will betray me, as I have betrayed,
> And I shall kiss the hand that does me wrong.
> But oh, not pardon—I need pardon more—
> But in proud torment, grim and unafraid,
> Burn in my hell nor cease the bitter song
> Your beauty triumphs in forevermore.[16]

Though he can forgive her, he will still be jealous and bitter
because he is not so immortal that he can overcome such emotions.
In fact, since he receives some sort of masochistic pleasure from the
hurts of love, the more he is wounded, the greater his love will have
to be in order to forgive. In "Love's Silence," he wants his Marna to
be free, to be true to herself and her soul, and to be ever ready to
have a new affair.

I do not ask your love as having rights
Because of all there is between us two.
Love has no rights, Love has but his delights,
Which but delight because they are not due.
The highest merit any man can prove
Is not enough to merit what Love gives,
And Love would lose its quality of love,
Lives it for any cause but that it lives.
Therefore I do not plead my gentle thought,
My foolish wisdom that would make you free.
My sacrifice, my broken heart be nought,
Even my great love itself, the best of me!
Martyr of Love, I see no other way
But to keep silence in your sight, and pray.[17]

Hovey was one of the first American writers to introduce modern attitudes about love into literature. American love poetry before him had been sentimental and idealistic; Hovey's lack of squeamishness allowed him to write about the body and physical involvement. His love poems reflect the rising sophistication of the 1890's: the flirtations of the Gibson Girl; the acceptance of divorce; and the recognition that physical passion is not an evil.

CHAPTER 8

Conclusion

WHAT Richard Hovey might have accomplished had he lived longer is, of course, an unanswerable question. His craftsmanship had shown a steady improvement over the years, and Hovey at thirty-five was a mature, disciplined, but still daring poet. Behind his work were the solid philosophical bases of political democracy and artistic integrity, and there can be no doubt that American literature is poorer because of his early death. On the other hand, that same early death probably inflated his reputation. Critics, remembering the fiasco made by their profession after the death of Keats, are somewhat cautious in judging the work of poets who die young; but the quality of Hovey's work was probably exaggerated by his peers. Moreover, Hovey was well known in critical and poetic circles; and his gregarious and warm-hearted personality had made him many friends.

In 1900, the year Hovey died, Edmund Clarence Stedman was preparing *An American Anthology*—an early collection of American poetry that strongly influenced subsequent critical opinion. Stedman included several of Hovey's lyrics, praised him in the biographical notes, and explained that Hovey had experienced a long internship and that death had come at the moment he was about to realize his powers. "He was ridding himself in a measure of certain affectations that told against him. . . . That his aim was high is shown even by his failures; and in his death there is no doubt that America has lost one of her best-equipped lyrical and dramatic writers."[1]

Other anthologists and critics followed the path started by Stedman, and Hovey's reputation began to build in the years immediately after 1900. Augustus White Long allowed four pages to Hovey's poetry in *American Poems* (1905), and Thomas Lounsbury gave him no fewer than ten pages in the *Yale Book of Verse* (1913).

Percy Boynton's *American Poets* (1918) contained several selections, including such long poems as "Spring" and "The Call of the Bugles." William Rose Benet included three lyrics in *Poems For Youth* (1925), and Alfred Kreymborg reprinted "A Stein Song" and "Unmanifest Destiny" in *Lyric America* (1930). To trace the growth of Hovey's reputation is to examine the several editions of Louis Untermeyer's popular anthology, *Modern American Poetry*. The first edition (1919) contained three Hovey poems; Untermeyer added one more to each following edition, until there were six in the fourth edition (1930); and these remained through the sixth edition (1942). But, when the seventh, or mid-century edition appeared in 1950, Hovey had been dropped completely.

Perhaps the best index to the rise and fall of Hovey's reputation can be found in a comparison of the two editions of *The Oxford Book of American Verse*. The first, published in 1927, contained ten pages of Hovey's poetry; the second (1950), edited by F. O. Matthiessen, had none. No doubt the number of pages devoted to Hovey in the first edition was swelled because Bliss Carman was its editor. Matthiessen's judgment is more correct. If the critic cared to make a general statement about Hovey's reputation, he could say that it reached its peak around 1930 and then went into gradual decline. Today, Hovey only has a place in a few children's anthologies. The "Sea Gypsy" and "At the Crossroads" are occasionally reprinted, but the half dozen or so of his lyrics that could be remembered have been forgotten.

Hovey's work, done during the 1890's, has many of the characteristics of twentieth-century American poetry. His use of free verse with short, uneven lines seems especially noteworthy; many of the Imagist poets would write in a similar style. The deliberate use of myth to convey contemporary problems, and the persona of the artist-hero are devices of modern poets that Hovey had used at an earlier time. In subject matter, he helped break the barriers that the Genteel Tradition had built against sex by presenting in his poetry modern attitudes about love. His translations and imitations of the French Symbolists helped to popularize that movement.

But Richard Hovey was not a major poet. Perhaps he experimented with too many different forms; and, as a consequence, his own style was late in developing. His early verses indicate too much concern for metrical exactness and rhyming regularity; the blank verse of the early Arthurian dramas is heavy and wooden. A reader today might have difficulty grasping Hovey's idealistic metaphysics; Stephen Crane's Naturalism seems more current. One also tires of encountering in poem after poem the same ideas of comradeship, love, drinking, and adventure. Although Hovey was familiar with the Symbolists, his own poetry achieves a symbolic level very seldom. Most of his poetry is direct statement phrased in rhythm and rhyme. It is pure lyric that contains little meaning beyond the surface intent. However, as Stedman mentioned, Hovey was acquiring more discipline, and his poetry seemed to be developing intensity of meaning. As it stands, it is unfortunate that the *Vagabondia* poems for which he is remembered are products of his early years.

It is difficult to assess how much actual influence Hovey had on later poets. His poems were popular at the turn of the century and were known to college students and others writing poetry. There is a direct influence on Robert Frost, who received inspiration from Hovey's example and career.[2] Whether there were similar influences on other poets cannot at this time be documented.

Richard Hovey remains a poet of some importance for the student of American literature and cultural history. In his writing one can discover techniques and styles that later greater poets were also to use. Modern American poetry was not born full-blown in 1914 with Amy Lowell, Ezra Pound, and the Imagist movement. There was an extensive period of development in which Hovey played a role—as a poet, a critic, and a personality. He was sensitive to the intellectual and social currents of his era, and his life and work provide a case study for tracing the development of twentieth-century ideas and trends.

The 1890's has been called "The Age of Contrasts," and Hovey's work reflects that variety. A list of the poets who influenced him indicates his complexity: Emerson and Baudelaire, Stevenson and Lanier, Whitman and Mallarmé, Kipling and Swinburne. Hovey himself could be as moral as Emerson and as decadent as Baudelaire; as romantic as Stevenson and as pious as Lanier; as real as Whitman and as foggy as Mallarmé; as imperialistic as Kipling and as sensuous as Swinburne. He seems to have possessed the mind of William Ernest Henley in the body of Oscar Wilde. The character of Richard Hovey provides an interesting example of complementarity: the ability of individuals to resolve or balance within themselves their opposing and contradictory forces of thought. He was not able to successfully resolve all the antitheses—Symbolism versus Realism, Imperialism or Socialism—but then no one else was either. Since many of the tensions working on Hovey confront people today, his life seems contemporary even though his poetry is forgotten. His spirit was present during the youth movement of the 1960's, and it can still be spotted in that long-haired, faunlike youth with the pack on his back who is heading west on Interstate 80. Richard Hovey is alive and well in America.

Notes and References

Chapter One

1. Allan Houston Macdonald, *Richard Hovey* (Durham, N.C., 1957), p. 11.
2. *Ibid.*, p. 38.
3. *Ibid.*, p. 43.
4. "Classnotes of '85," *Dartmouth Literary Monthly*, III (October, 1888), 47.
5. Macdonald, p. 52.
6. *To the End of the Trail* (New York, 1908), p. 3.
7. Macdonald, p. 56.
8. "Chronicle and Comment," *The Bookman*, VIII (December, 1898), 307.
9. Bliss Carman, "Preface," *The Holy Graal and Other Fragments by Richard Hovey*, edited with Introduction and notes by Mrs. Richard Hovey (New York, 1907), p. 9.
10. Macdonald, p. 123.
11. *Daily Tatler*, 5 Nov., 1896, p. 2.
12. Macdonald, p. 143.
13. *Songs from Vagabondia* (Boston, 1894), p. 54.
14. Louis Untermeyer, *Modern American Poetry*, 3rd. ed. (New York, 1925), p. 10.
15. Macdonald, p. 155.
16. Frederick W. Robertson, *Lectures on the Influence of Poetry and Wordsworth* (London, 1906), p. 55.
17. *More Songs from Vagabondia* (Boston, 1896), p. 27.
18. Richard Hovey, *A Poem and Three Letters* (Hanover, N.H., 1935), n.p.
19. Macdonald, p. 210.
20. "The Strenuous Life," *Works of Theodore Roosevelt* (New York, 1900), XII, 7.
21. *The Marriage of Guenevere* (Chicago, 1895), p. 117.
22. *Along the Trail* (Boston, 1898), p. 104.
23. *Ibid.*

Chapter Two

1. *Songs from Vagabondia*, p. 1.
2. *Ibid.*, p. 14.

3. *Ibid.*, p. 45.
4. *Ibid.*, p. 9.
5. *Ibid.*, p. 19.
6. *Ibid.*, pp. 22–23.
7. *Ibid.*, p. 33.
8. *Ibid.*, pp. 36–37.
9. *Ibid.*, pp. 41–43.
10. *Ibid.*, pp. 27–29.

Chapter Three

1. *More Songs from Vagabondia*, p. 1.
2. *Ibid.*, p. 7.
3. *Ibid.*, p. 13.
4. Carman, "How Hovey Wrote 'Barney McGee'," *The Bookman*, XLII (January, 1916), 561.
5. *More Songs from Vagabondia*, p. 22.
6. *Ibid.*, p. 25.
7. *Ibid.*, p. 63.
8. *Ibid.*, p. 31.
9. *Ibid.*, p. 32.
10. *Ibid.*, p. 33.
11. *Ibid.*, p. 34.
12. *Ibid.*, pp. 35–38.
13. *Ibid.*, p. 58.
14. *Ibid.*, p. 59.
15. *Ibid.*, p. 71.
16. *Ibid.*, p. 72.

Chapter Four

1. Carman, "Preface," *The Holy Graal*, p. 9.
2. *The Holy Graal*, p. 23.
3. *The Quest of Merlin* (New York, 1891), p. 15.
4. *Ibid.*, p. 16.
5. *Ibid.*, p. 74.
6. *Ibid.*, p. 79.
7. *The Marriage of Guenevere*, pp. 40–42.
8. *Ibid.*, p. 63.
9. *Ibid.*, p. 138.
10. Mrs. Hovey, "Introduction," *The Holy Graal*, p. 14.
11. *The Birth of Galahad* (Boston, 1898), p. 21.

12. *Ibid.*, p. 31.
13. *Taliesin* (Boston, 1899), p. 5.
14. *Ibid.*, p. 19.
15. *Ibid.*, p. 30.
16. *Ibid.*, p. 57.
17. Mrs. Hovey, "Introduction," *The Holy Graal*, p. 10.
18. Curtis Hidden Page, "Richard Hovey's *Taliesin*—A Poet's Poem," *The Bookman*, XI (April, 1900), 131.
19. Mrs. Hovey's note, *The Holy Graal*, p. 57.
20. *The Holy Graal*, p. 119.
21. Mrs. Hovey, "Introduction," *The Holy Graal*, p. 18.
22. Curtis Hidden Page, "The Plays and Poems of Richard Hovey," *The Bookman*, VIII (December, 1898), 360.
23. *Taliesin*, p. 9.
24. *Merlin*, p. 31.
25. *The Holy Graal*, p. 119.
26. *The Marriage of Guenevere*, p. 170.
27. *The Holy Graal*, p. 41.
28. *The Marriage of Guenevere*, p. 90.
29. *The Holy Graal*, p. 70.
30. *The Birth of Galahad*, p. 21.
31. *The Holy Graal*, p. 48.
32. *The Birth of Galahad*, p. 21.
33. *Taliesin*, p. 5.
34. "Maeterlinck as a Prophet of Joy," *The Bookman*, IX (March, 1899), 65.

Chapter Five

1. *Along the Trail*, pp. 3–5.
2. *Ibid.*, p. 5.
3. *Ibid.*, pp. 17–18.
4. *Ibid.*, p. 25.
5. *Ibid.*, p. 27.
6. *Ibid.*, p. 29.
7. *Ibid.*, pp. 33–34.
8. *Ibid.*, pp. 34–35.
9. *Ibid.*, pp. 39–40.
10. Macdonald, p. 129.
11. *Along the Trail*, pp. 79–80.
12. *Ibid.*, pp. 66–67.
13. *Ibid.*, p. 76.
14. *Ibid.*, p. 78.

15. *Ibid.*, pp. 69–77.
16. Macdonald, p. 130.
17. *Along the Trail*, pp. 79–80.
18. *A Poem and Three Letters*, n.p.
19. Carman, "How Hovey Wrote 'Barney McGee'," *The Bookman*, XLII (January, 1916), 561.
20. "Dr. Edward H. Allen '85, Oldest Living Graduate will be 100 this month," *Dartmouth Alumni Magazine*, LVI (April, 1964), 11.
21. *Along the Trail*, p. 55.
22. *Ibid.*, p. 93.
23. *Ibid.*, p. 95.
24. *Ibid.*, pp. 98–99.
25. *Ibid.*, p. 100.
26. *Ibid.*
27. *To the End of the Trail*, p. 14.
28. *Along the Trail*, pp. 102–103.
29. *Ibid.*, pp. 103–104.

Chapter Six

1. *Last Songs from Vagabondia* (Boston, 1900), pp. 1–2.
2. *Ibid.*, pp. 49–50.
3. *Ibid.*, p. 50.
4. *Ibid.*, p. 15.
5. *Ibid.*, pp. 16–18.
6. *Ibid.*, p. 72.
7. *Ibid.*, p. 52.
8. *Ibid.*, p. 51.
9. *Ibid.*, p. 35.
10. *Ibid.*, pp. 38–40.
11. *Ibid.*, pp. 68–70.
12. *Ibid.*, pp. 37–38.
13. *Ibid.*, p. 54.
14. *Ibid.*, p. 49.
15. *Ibid.*, p. 51.
16. *Ibid.*, pp. 78–79.

Chapter Seven

1. *To the End of the Trail*, p. 35.
2. *Ibid.*, p. 17.
3. *Ibid.*, p. 45.

4. "Preface," *The Plays of Maurice Maeterlinck* (Chicago, 1894), p. 4.

5. "Chronicle and Comment," *The Bookman*, VIII (December, 1898), 308.

6. *Ibid.*

7. *To the End of the Trail*, p. 139.

8. *Ibid.*, p. 134.

9. *Ibid.*, p. 114.

10. *Ibid.*, p. 116.

11. *Ibid.*, p. 118.

12. *Ibid.*, p. 121.

13. *Ibid.*, p. 128.

14. *Ibid.*, p. 123.

15. *Ibid.*

16. *Ibid.*, p. 144.

17. *Ibid.*, pp. 147–48.

Chapter Eight

1. Edmund Clarence Stedman, *An American Anthology* (Boston, 1900), p. 801.

2. Lawrance Thompson, *Robert Frost: The Early Years* (New York, 1966), p. 143.

Selected Bibliography

PRIMARY SOURCES

(listed in chronological order)
Poetry and Translation

Launcelot and Guenevere: A Poem in Dramas. New York: United States
Book Company, 1891.
Seaward: An Elegy on the Death of Thomas William Parsons. Boston: D.
Lothrop Company, 1893.
Songs from Vagabondia (with Bliss Carman). Boston: Copeland and Day,
1894.
The Plays of Maurice Maeterlinck. Chicago: Stone & Kimball, 1894.
The Marriage of Guenevere. Chicago: Stone & Kimball, 1895.
The Plays of Maurice Maeterlinck–Second Series. Chicago: Stone & Kim-
ball, 1896.
More Songs from Vagabondia (with Bliss Carman). Boston: Copeland and
Day, 1896.
The Birth of Galahad. Boston: Small, Maynard and Company, 1898.
Along the Trail. Boston: Small, Maynard and Company, 1898.
Taliesin. Boston: Small, Maynard and Company, 1899.
Last Songs from Vagabondia (with Bliss Carman). Boston: Small, Maynard
and Company, 1900.
The Holy Graal and Other Fragments. Edited with Introduction and Notes
by Mrs. Richard Hovey. New York: Duffield & Company, 1907.
To the End of the Trail. Edited with Notes by Mrs. Richard Hovey. New
York: Duffield & Company, 1908.
Dartmouth Lyrics. Edited by Edwin Osgood Grover. Boston: Small,
Maynard & Company, 1924.

Essays

"The Dying Century," *Dartmouth Literary Magazine*, II (February, 1888),
208–11.
"Delsarte and Poetry," *Independent*, XLIII (August 27, 1891), 1267.
"The Technique of Poetry," *Independent*, XLIV (April 7 and 21, 1892), 473,
544.
"On the Threshold," *Independent*, XLIV (November 3, 1892), 1546–47.

"The Technique of Rhyme," *Independent*, XLV (October 19, 1893), 1399.
"The Elements of Poetic Technique," *Independent*, XLVI (September 27 and October 4, 1894), 1241, 1275.
"The Passing of Realism," *Independent*, XLVII (August 22, 1895), 1125.
"Maeterlinck as a Prophet of Joy," *The Bookman*, IX (March, 1899), 64.

SECONDARY SOURCES

CARMAN, BLISS. "Richard Hovey, My Friend," *Criterion*, XXIII (April, 1900), 527. Appreciation of Hovey as a man.
———. "How Hovey Wrote 'Barney McGee'," *The Bookman*, XLII (January, 1916), 561. Explanation of how Hovey, the poet, worked.
CLEAVES, F. P. "Richard Hovey,—Barnstormer!" *Dartmouth Alumni Magazine*, XXI (March, 1929), 294–98. Relates episodes of Hovey's early career.
MACDONALD, ALLAN. "Charles Edward Hovey," *Dartmouth Alumni Magazine*, XXXIX (April, 1947), 21–23. About the poet's father.
———. *Richard Hovey: Man & Craftsman*. Durham, N.C.: Duke University Press, 1957. Only complete study of Hovey; based upon letters and other original materials; excellent primary and secondary bibliography.
MARCHAND, ERNEST. "Hovey's First Flight," *Dartmouth Alumni Magazine*, XXXI (June, 1939), 15–16. Describes Hovey's first book of lyrics, which appeared in 1880.
MATULKA, BARBARA. "Letters of Mallarmé and Maeterlinck to Richard Hovey," *Romantic Review*, XVIII (July–Sept., 1927), 232–37.
PAGE, CURTIS HIDDEN. "The Plays and Poems of Richard Hovey," *The Bookman*, VIII (December, 1898), 360. Earliest appreciation of Hovey as an artist.
———. "Richard Hovey's *Taliesin*—A Poet's Poem," *The Bookman*, XI (April, 1900), 131. Sensitive review of Hovey's best long work.
PATTERSON, WALTER B. "Reminiscences of Richard Hovey," *Dartmouth Literary Magazine*, XXIV (May, 1910), 223–25.
STEDMAN, E. C. *An American Anthology*. Boston: Mifflin, 1900. Pages 800–801 contain a warm appreciation of Hovey's talent.
UNTERMEYER, LOUIS. *Modern American Poetry*, 3rd. ed. New York: Harcourt, Brace & Co., 1925. Pages 10–12 contain critical doubts about the value of the *Vagabondias*.
VON ENDE, AMELIE. "The Ethical Message of Richard Hovey's Poem in Dramas," *Poet Lore*, XX (January, 1909), 69–76. Explication of the Arthurian plays.

Index

(The works of Hovey are listed under his name)